Living Colors

Anonymous Artists

Some of the earliest palettes from the ancient and medieval periods. The work of great, but often unrecorded, artists and artisans of the past who, while working within conventional traditions, succeeded in leaving behind some of the simplest but most striking color schemes the world has ever seen.

1 | Egyptian Painted Decoratives

As in many periods before the Renaissance, there was no cult of the artist in ancient Egypt. Painters were part of a team of craftsmen and were known as "outline scribes," a term implying they also doubled as hieroglyph writers.

Perhaps because these anonymous painters were not encouraged to develop individual styles, the 3,000-odd years of tomb painting in Pharaonic Egypt offers a remarkably consistent palette, even if combinations were always changing. Though limited, the range of colors was entirely adequate for an art developed not for realistic portrayal but rather to convey a message, half in words or hieroglyphs, and half in pictures, to indicate the dead person's worth and his prospects in the afterlife.

Colors were often used for symbolic or conventional reasons; for instance, men were at times identified with deep red ocher skin tones and women with yellow ocher. Most importantly, however, no other palette, simple or complex, was ever so clearly representative of a landscape, namely, the Nile valley: the yellow-red of the desert, the blue of the river, the green of papyrus, and the palest blue of the subtropical sky.

Pigments all came from mineral sources. Together with the ochers, a strong yellow came from orpiment (a sulphide of arsenic), white from gypsum, black from soot, and blue from an artificial frit of silica, copper, and calcium finely ground, and sometimes from Afghan lapis lazuli. Green was made by mixing the frit with yellow, a process that accounts for its bluish undertone, and occasionally by incorporating the more expensive pigment of pure malachite. Exposed to occasional dampness, blue and green have had a tendency to "rust" slightly over the millennia, and the original colors may have been brighter than shown here.

Paintings were generally executed on plaster covered with a thin wash of color as background. During the Old Kingdom (c. 3200-2200 BC), and occasionally later, this was a bluish gray, and during the New Kingdom (1580-663 BC) a stark white and even a strong yellow, as in many of the tombs at Thebes. After an outline had been provided in red ocher, colors were applied flat, built up in layers as they dried, with almost no texture, except some stippling on robes, as befits a *naïf* perspectival treatment. As they are tempera paints mixed with water soluble gums, they have a matte, opaque quality. The last step was the addition of black outlines to clarify the figures.

A Moveable Red

Heavily dependent on the local ocher source, red is the most variable color, a warm earthy brown in Theban tombs and an almost purple red at the Kharga oasis. Along with black, blue and green are the predominant accent colors and can be used almost interchangeably, given how close their tones are, although remarkable depictions of verdant foliage are achieved with combinations of several greens, ranging from olive to blue-green, on painted wooden funeral caskets. The essence of Egyptian color usage is three-to four-color combinations hinged on red or yellow.

The colors shown here are taken from tempera copies painted on the spot in Egypt by artists accompanying archaeological teams. They are among the best surviving records of the original paintings, which, along with the plaster-work, have degraded considerably since the tombs were opened.

The god Osiris, symbol of eternal life, and three attendants, from the Tomb of Nebamum and Ipuky, Thebes, c. 1380 BC. Tempera on paper, copy of tempera on plaster original. Egyptian Expedition of the Metropolitan Museum of Art, Rogers Fund, 1930. (30.4.157) © 1978 by The Metropolitan Museum of Art

2 | Sophisticated Greek Earthtones

The best, and for a long time the only, known Greek palette is the one fired indelibly in ceramics: the earthtones. The absence of stronger hues—blues, greens, yellows—has prompted some speculation in recent centuries: Were the Greeks all color blind (see footnote)? Were good pigments unavailable? Did Greek painters, whose naturalism was so different from Egypt's stylized art, find color a distracting nuisance?

It is now known that ancient Greek painters inherited the full range of Egyptian pigments, and even added some new ones of their own, notably lead-based white and red. Since these were used everywhere—in paintings, on marble sculptures and even on temples, where blue, red, black, yellow, green, and gold emphasized the various parts of the building such as cornices and carved metopes—the reason for the relatively restricted palette of ceramics is partly technical.

At the height of their art, around the sixth and fifth centuries BC, Greek potters had perfected techniques of using slips of clay, ground more or less finely, and repeated firings at different temperatures to achieve a range of colors from buff to red and black. The further firings, often at high temperatures, needed for color glazes would have at least compromised, if not completely destroyed, these exquisite tones. There is an aesthetic consideration, too: Any strong color

Nicosthenes, cup decorated with Greek sailing ships, Louvre, Paris, c. 510 BC. Sophisticated designs generated with only the colors available from slips of clay, ground to different fineness. Giraudon/ Art Resource, New York.

visually overwhelms this subtle palette when, from the mid-fifth century on, statuettes and *lekythoi* (small vases for holding sweet-smelling oils) intended for tombs were decorated with vegetable-based tempera paints after the final firing, the matte greens and pastel tints of blue, yellow, purple, and pink were almost always applied over a white ground only.

The best ceramics came from around Athens. The dominant tones were those of iron- and manganese-rich clays available locally, most notably an orangy brown terra-cotta, extended by extraordinary control (given the primitive nature of their wood-fired kilns) of temperature and humidity to include ocher yellow, soft mauves, and burnished reds and oranges, a few of which are shown here, as well as black. In the original black-figure style, the slip that would turn black in firing was used to paint the designs on the unglazed surface; the process was reversed around 525 BC with the slip used instead to fill in the background and to draw details (red-figure style), a much easier process.

From Pots to Walls

Apparently this palette was also used for interiors. Excavations at Olynthus have revealed rooms painted from corner to corner with fully saturated shades of red and yellow, often set off by zones of black—a style that may well have influenced Pompeiian wall painting (see page 7). Today, especially in northern climates, such density of color could be oppressive and is considered more appropriate for furniture. The colors were used successfully, however, during the nineteenth-century classical revival to pick out architectural detail, most notably on the stately exterior of London's Albert Hall. The rich tobacco browns and earthy reds also harmonized with the favorite Victorian medium of brick.

This palette can generate many different analogous harmonies of earth-tones. No single color need be particularly dominant, though combinations should include cream at the center and use black as an accent. The colors are substantial, serious, even masculine.

William Ewert Gladstone, Studies in Homer and the Homeric Age. *Gladstone (1809–1898), Britain's prime minister from 1868 to 1874, based his theory largely on studying Greek literature, which surprisingly never refers to the color blue, except occasionally with the vague word* kyanos, *sky-colored, and by describing the sea as* oinopa, *or wine-colored. It is thought highly improbable, however, that the ancients perceived color any differently than we do.*

Now that even purple clothes our walls, no famous picture is painted. We must believe that when the painter's equipment was less complete, the results were in every respect better.

—Pliny, Natural History, XXXV, 50

3 | Pompeii's Mural Exotics

The lament of Roman historian Pliny the Elder (AD 23–79), one that echoes down to our own over-colored age, is all the more poignant since he died in Pompeii—a favored Roman resort town now famous for its bright color—during the cataclysmic eruption of Mount Vesuvius on August 24, AD 79.

Sealed for centuries under a thick layer of ash and lava, Pompeii's hidden splendors were gradually revealed in excavations starting in 1709. Most spectacular are the well-preserved murals that variously influenced decorative tastes in the eighteenth and nineteenth centuries and inspired many artists, architects, furniture makers, and potters from the Adam brothers and Fontaine (see Enriched Classicism for Empires, p. 48) to Owen Jones.

The paintings range from early illusionistic landscapes in naturalistic colors, to the more decorative later styles, in which trompe l'oeil architectural details, trailing vines, slender candelabra and abstract geometric motifs frame smaller still lifes and mythological scenes. These are characterized by dramatic color blocking in super-rich tones of red, green, deep brown, dark purple, and, above all, black.

Classic Brights
Whereas the earlier palettes were soft, with gentle shades of green, mauve, and yellow on a blue-gray ground, the later palette is all energy and noise—not inappropriate for a summer seaside resort. In fact, the warmth the colors engendered partly made up for the restricted light from windows facing in on central courtyards. Adding to their effect,

Jason Before Pelias. From Casa di Iasone, Pompeii, first century AD. Fresco. A palette of pales, including the distinctive light blue, blue-green, and purple, that was to be picked up in the Empire Style almost two millennia later. Erich Lessing/Art Resource, New York.

the earth and mineral pigments used were mixed in a solution of lime and soap with a little added wax; after painting, the surface was burnished with a metal trowel or marble roller and then buffed with a cloth to achieve a deep shine.

The Lustration, from the Villa of Mysteries, Pompeii, c. AD 60. Silenus plays a lyre in honor of the dead Dionysos, part of a series of frescoes dedicated to the god in one room of a suburban villa outside the main city. A density of color that was probably imported from Greece, where such strong colors are also known to have been used for the interiors of wealthier homes. Scala/Art Resource, New York.

Most distinctive are the brilliant reds, generally the cool bluish tones of cinnabar and madder lakes but also some warm Etruscan earth reds. Though it was not unusual to paint a whole room, including ceiling, just in red, one of the most successful harmonies from the Villa of Mysteries (shown here) complemented red with a blue-green. The use of ocher yellow and purplish brown serve to enrich the overall scheme, which remains one of the most sophisticated uses of brights ever to be developed.

4 | **Coptic Woven Paintings**

The Copts (from *Kipt*, Arabic corruption of *Aigyptios*, the Greek word for Egypt) are descendents of the ancient Egyptians, who adopted Christianity in the first century AD and refused Islamic conversion after the Arab conquest. Some three million Copts still live in Egypt. They are best known for the extraordinary fabric pictures of the fourth to twelfth centuries AD, many of which have been well preserved by the arid air of the desert regions to which the Copts were often forced to retreat.

Horseman holding a staff, Coptic, c. fifth century AD. Linen and wool tapestry. Remarkably well preserved—the original madder red can be seen on the lips and behind the head—this fragment shows a palette of colors from plant and animal dyes similar to that of Middle Eastern kilims. Courtesy The Kanebo Collection, Osaka.

Common Coptic images were stylized depictions of animals, birds, and mythological figures, and flat renderings of foliage, illustrating Greek and Near Eastern as well as Egyptian influences. That some of these designs include naturalistic, frontal portraits of people is all the more remarkable since often the fabrics were not embroideries but genuine tapestry weaves executed on looms.

Textile's Oldest Palette

The weavers were adept at working with both undyed linen—generally for the warp, which had to be strong—and dyed wool yarns—for the weft in which the design was built up, one line at a time. Wool, unlike linen, dyes easily, and was colored with many of the same vegetable and animal dyes that have been used on Middle Eastern carpets (see Kilims of Anatolia, p. 60) right up to the twentieth century. These include indigo and woad for blue, madder root, and to a lesser extent kermes and lac—which came from Armenia and India respectively and were far more expensive—for red, and weld, saffron, or pomegranate flowers for yellow. Purple came from a mix of red and blue; green from yellow with blue; and pink from diluted red.

Red does not have quite the dominant role or symbolic force in Coptic textiles that it does in the carpets, largely because of the generous use of the unbleached creamy white of linen widely available in Egypt for the background of the images. Nevertheless, the weavers revealed a preference for dark and saturated modalities by favoring deep greens, purples, and reds, many of which have now degenerated to maroons and rusts, and using orange, yellow, green, and blue more as accents.

Puttae surrounding central roundel depicting man with captive, Coptic, c. sixth century AD. Linen and wool tapestry. The background is linen, while the design is executed in wool, which takes dyes easily. Courtesy The Kanebo Collection, Osaka.

Because wool yarn is bulkier than linen, the pictures tended to stand up a little above the linen background, giving an illusion of relief. The gentle gradations of tone that are common with natural dyes give the fabrics an unprecedented richness.

5 | Bayeux Tapestry's Medieval Tints

This work records the last successful invasion of Britain, that by William the Conqueror, a Norman duke from the northwest coast of France. Shown in the eighty-foot by three-foot hanging is a detailed, play-by-play account of the events leading up to the decisive battle against the English king Harold at Hastings on October 28, 1066.

Not actually a tapestry, but rather an embroidery on linen, it was most likely commissioned by William's half-brother Odo, Bishop of Bayeux, and stitched around 1088 by English seamstresses famous for such work. It is a unique color record, since for centuries it was only displayed once a year and remained folded up the rest of the time. The colors have survived almost without any fading and show a palette that evolved during the Dark Ages.

The design and the colors used are remarkably consistent throughout despite the number of hands that must have labored on it, indicating a carefully planned project with a single *auteur* responsible for the design. The five principle colors are terra-cotta, a grayish blue-green, an old gold (yellow-tan), olive green, and a deep blue with a slight but definite greenish tinge. Also appearing are a soft sage green and dark, almost black, blue, a color the embroiderers apparently ran out of two thirds of the way through the project.

Abstraction of Color

With its thick woolen threads laid and couched on fine off-white linen, the effect is of masses of light and shade. The colors are not used naturalistically, with horses and clothing alike shown arbitrarily in yellow, blue, red, or green. There is no attempt at flesh tones, or portraiture, in the caricatured faces.

Nevertheless, the whole is executed with painterly skill, using broad swaths of color and some modeling of details such as horses' musculature in contrasting colors, possibly in imitation of the wall painting that figured in Romanesque church decoration. It is a fine example of color used to enhance a sense of tension and movement. Stylistic or symbolic rules governing which colors should be placed where are not evident (as they were in Egyptian murals), and colors were used and combined freely, creating an impression of far more hues than actually exist in this very simple palette. The predominance, however, of combinations of blue with yellow and terra-cotta with green do show a developed sense of color balance and harmony.

Bayeux Tapestry, Musée de la Tapisserie, Bayeux, c. 1085 depicting Norman knights fallen under the hill of Seulac during William the Conqueror's invasion of Britain in 1066. Like Coptic work, the medium is plain linen and dyed wool, but the well-preserved colors are relatively delicate in tone. Scala/Art Resource, New York.

6 | Stained Glass Spirituals

A feature of medieval stained glass is its incomparable purity of color. The palette was dominated by the basic, primary, and generally strongest colors—red, blue (almost always the background color at that time), and yellow—with secondary green, which glaziers apparently could not get to full saturation, and mauve used largely for detailing.

The technique of making windows of colored glass dates back to fourth century Constantinople. Since "Let there be light" were God's first words in the Bible, this made stained glass especially appealing to church leaders, and colors, like every detail of the world around them, were construed as a sign of God's presence on earth: red for the blood of Christ and martyrdom; blue for heaven and piety, yellow or gold for light and His glory, and green for faith and immortality. The windows, according to the Abbé Suger, builder of arguably the first truly Gothic cathedral, St. Denis in Paris, let in light "to illumine men's minds so that they may travel through it to an apprehension of God's light."

Flashing Color

Most of the colors were originally an accidental byproduct of the use of beechwood ash in glass manufacture, which lowers the melting point of sand and aids fusion. Varying percentages of iron and manganese found naturally in the ash, along with careful temperature control, eventually allowed glaziers to conjure up a brilliant range of blues, greens, browns, pinks, and purples. Dark blue and red needed the addition of copper and zinc (probably from brass filings) and sometimes cobalt, while the strong yellow stain was produced by painting and then firing silver sulphide on the back of white glass. The red was so strong that at the thickness of glass then being made it came out practically black; it was thus the only color often applied—"flashed"—as a thin glass layer onto a colorless glass base. Design details, such as faces or drapery, were painted on with iron oxide grays and browns that were then also fixed to the glass by firing.

Most stained glass pictures, until the introduction in the sixteenth century of colored enamels for painting on plain glass, were built up like a mosaic. Holding the pieces of glass together are strips of lead that are H-shaped in cross section. These visually outline the colors in black, increasing their apparent brilliance and sharpening the images when seen from a distance. As it is, the depth and richness of the colors can hardly be done justice on paper.

A sybil and prophet, from St. Pierre, Chartres, thirteenth century. Incomparable blues were the trademark of the French glaziers of Chartres's cathedral and churches. Erich Lessing/Art Resource, New York

7 | **Russian Icons—Byzantine Traditions**

Icons, from the Greek word (*eikon*) for image, are devotional portraits of Christ, angels, or saints common in the Greek or Russian Orthodox Church. Icons may have evolved from Egypto-Roman portrait panels, often commemorating someone deceased; their development was a Byzantine phenomenon, but reached its peak in the magnificent Russian tradition of the fourteenth to sixteenth centuries. At the end of that period, Tsar Peter the Great (1672–1725), a committed westernizer, introduced reforms that eradicated much of the eastern influences in Russian culture, resulting in the decline of the art of Russian icons.

Icons are extremely formal in composition: figures are arranged or poised to fit basic, and religiously significant, geometric shapes, such as the triangle for the Trinity, and the circle for eternal life. With little shading except for skin tones, colors are blocked strongly with a hierarchical look reminiscent of mosaics, an evident influence. In addition, color takes on a supremely symbolic importance— it was in icons that the tradition was established that the Virgin Mary always wore a blue robe, the color of heaven and of truth. Gold, the ultimate emblem of God's light (sometimes replaced by yellow paint), and silver were by far the most important colors, applied in leaf form for the backgrounds or as *rizas*, stamped metal sheet coverings which left only the faces and hands visible.

Russian icons were usually executed on wood boards with tempera paints. The board was prepared with gesso and polished smooth to give the paints a luminous quality. Usually red paint was used to draw the picture according to the *Podliniki* or authorized versions. As in most icons, gold predominates, even to the point where the painting was often executed over a gold leaf ground, giving the colors the effect of being lit from behind.

A New Direction

Andrei Roublev (c. 1370-1430), the finest Russian icon painter and one of the few to be known by name, was able to take the color potential of this medium to a new level. In arrangement, his icons are clearly influenced by Byzantine style, but the figures are far more fluid. The color scale, too, is brighter, more complex, different in key, and distinctively Russian. By any other hand, the use of orange, vermilion, and turquoise, as shown here (the background is heavily damaged), might easily have assumed a primitive garishness of folk art. Instead the controlled intensity of these tones becomes an essential part of the composition.

Andrei Roublev, *Old Testament Trinity*, c. 1410–20. Tretyakov Gallery, Moscow. Tempera on wood. More fluid than Byzantine icons, with more sophisticated colors, Roublev's work marks a high point in the development of Christian religious art. Scala/Art Resource, New York.

Subsequent icon painting in Russia, which dominated production after the sack of Constantinople in 1453 by the Turks, largely continued Roublev's development. Colors were used in a predictable manner: golds and silvers and to a lesser extent lighter yellows, reds, and greens for backgrounds; reds and pinks and green-blues for drama, often to color robes; white on horses and garments as startling accent effects; and black for outlining. This somberly substantial palette of warm tones, punctuated by elegant white, blue-green, and orange, is underutilized by modern colorists.

8 | **Illuminated Prayer Books**

Typical of medieval manuscripts are exotic illustrations used to accompany the text, not only embellishing but also literally illuminating or shedding light on the meaning of the words. A Book of Hours, such as the *Très Riches Heures* of the Duke of Berry from which this palette is taken, was a small book (often only four by five inches) that could be easily carried around by its owner. Part calendar, part prayer book, it contained psalms and prayers appropriate to the saints who supposedly governed each hour of the day, as well as illustrations (not always colored) to aid in devotion. Between the late-thirteenth and mid-sixteenth centuries in Europe they were runaway best-sellers, easily outselling the Bible.

The *Très Riches Heures* was the last and finest work painted by the Limbourg brothers, Pol, Jean and Herman, who all died of the plague along with their patron, Jean, the Duke of Berry in 1416. Their illustration represents an important return to realism, which had not been used in illuminated manuscripts since the sixth century. In contrast to the stylized colorways of Romanesque or earlier Gothic manuscripts, colors of objects from horses to roofs are naturalistic, the sky is shaded convincingly from a deep ultramarine above to pale blue at the horizon, and aerial perspective—in which distant landscape is given a blue tinge—is a favorite device.

A Pigment More Expensive than Gold

Applied to the finest calfskin vellum, the pigments used include ultramarine (blue), verdigris and malachite (green), red lead and kermes lake (red), and orpiment (yellow). The use of blue, which gives an impression of great depth, is particularly striking because, coming from a single mine in Afghanistan, this pigment was more expensive than gold. Blue's elevated role, and the frequent use of gold scrollwork, stars, and other patterns, make a strong allusion to the French royal coat-of-arms—gold fleur-de-lys on a blue ground—particularly important to the Duke, who was the third son of Jean le Bon, King of France.

Key to the palette is this rich, almost purplish blue, used in relatively generous quantities. From this follows a gentle diminuendo of tones through slate blue (roofs), pale blue (sky, horizon), very pale gray-green and pink (architecture), and a soft verdigris, or blue-green (landscape). Against this, the perfectly controlled accents of vermilion, orange, coral pink, or yellow heighten a luminosity that is uncanny given that most of the colors are slightly grayed.

Pol de Limbourg, *The Purification,* from the *Très Riches Heures* du Duc de Berry, c. 1415. Musée Condé, Chantilly. Hand-painted and hand-written at first, such prayer books were the bestsellers of their day, though only the wealthiest could afford lavish illustration of this quality, where not even a single shadow is allowed to mar the clarity of the colors. Note the generous use of an exquisite ultramarine, the most expensive pigment at the time. Giraudon/Art Resource.

9 | Unicorn Tapestries—End of an Era

The Hunt of the Unicorn tapestries represent the climax, and the end, of the Gothic tradition. At the time they were woven in northern Europe, around 1495–1505, the Renaissance with its rediscovered classicism was well under way in Italy.

Unlike the Bayeux, these are true tapestries and were woven on location for feudal lords by itinerant weavers to enhance bleak castle walls as well as to keep out drafts. One of the great values of such tapestries in an age of upheavals and migrations was that they could be easily rolled up and moved. Originally custom-designed for specific spots—the Unicorn series is of medium size, with panels around eight by twelve feet, and so was probably for a bedchamber—they were unfortunately often mutilated to fit round doors and windows in their new locations.

Composed of uncolored warp, or vertical, threads, the tapestry's palette appears in the weft threads which are predominantly wool, a material that can be dyed to almost incomparable depth and richness. Silk and silver-gilt threads are used also, particularly for shiny highlights. Remarkably, only three dyes were used to produce the full range of colors: madder for red, weld for yellow and brown, and woad for blue. The use of different mordants to fix the dyes allowed the expansion of the color range: aluminum and zinc for reds from bright ruby and purplish red to clove pink; the same mordants with a mixture of madder and weld for midnight blue; and copper with weld and woad for the greens.

Forest Tones

The colors show the influence of Flemish art, and the original cartoon design may have been done by an artist from Flanders, Belgium. The predominant blue-green of the background is a compilation of deep blue, blue-gray, forest green, and pale yellow-green. (This contrasts with *The Lady and the Unicorn* tapestries in Paris's Cluny museum, which use a pink-red background.) Bold accents of red, a favorite color of the Middle Ages, in flowers, fruit, and clothing provide the decorative touch that defines Gothic. While perspective is played down, three-dimensional modeling of figures and flora is achieved by inlaying lighter tones on darker colors. Since hatching is a very complex process in a picture that is built up line by line, weavers often took short cuts by shading with flat areas of the lighter tone.

Today the colors have faded and, in the case of the reds, have blued a little with time. The original colors can be seen on the back, which has been unexposed to light. We can still appreciate the enormous richness of the all-over design and the color that fills every part of the pictures; creamy

The Hunt of the Unicorn, The Unicorn Defends Himself, Franco-Flemish c. 1500. Symbol of the Virgin Mary, the white unicorn represented purity, virtue, and kingship. Silk, wool, silver, and silver-gilt threads. The Metropolitan Museum of Art, Gift of John D. Rockefeller, Jr., The Cloisters Collection, 1937. (37.80.4) © 1988 by The Metropolitan Museum of Art

white is used not for background but as an active element for skin tones and for the central symbolic figure of the unicorn, which represents purity and kingship.

By using the dark green and blue predominantly for the background, the lighter colors are thrown forward in sharp relief, and white itself becomes an accent. The fully saturated magenta red that is used as the other accent is a strong complement to the green, but its bluish tinge maintains the palette's cool tonality. Note these are the basic tapestry colors that were revived by William Morris in the late-nineteenth century and are still a popular choice for upholstery.

Heroes of the Renaissance

The elegant palettes of the Italian Renaissance, a time when painters were emerging as the intellectual equals of scientists and writers and were able to break free from the traditions of icon painting and other arts to develop their own idiosyncratic visions. Particularly significant is the development of oil painting by van Eyck and Leonardo, a revolutionary technique that brought in a new range of rich and subtle tones.

10 | Duccio di Buoninsegna

Duccio's color palette is a remarkable demonstration of the brilliant colors that can be achieved with only mineral pigments. The pink which characterizes his series of altar panels, the *Maestà* (1285–1311), for Siena Cathedral seems as vivid as any vermilion, yet is produced simply by mixing an exceptionally bright red earth with white. Similarly, the green of terra verde is an earth pigment of particular strength that he obtained locally.

Duccio (c. 1255–1319), whose workshop was to dominate the art of Siena for many years, was one of the earliest painters to be influenced by classical painting, demonstrated by (still slightly crude) illusionistic tricks of perspective. He nevertheless owed much to traditions of Byzantine and Gothic religious painting and his *Maestà*, like his other work, makes use of the rich effects of gold leaf for backgrounds and halos. Across the limitless but abstract space implied by the gilt is splashed the concrete harmony of the pink and gray architecture with its bold, simple planes.

Accenting this basic three-color scheme are roughly six jewel-like colors from emerald green to deep blue, for which Duccio used only the highest quality ultramarine, and a range of browns. Still influenced by the Byzantine icon tradition, and unlike Piero della Francesca's progressions a century later, these colors are used simply and monolithically to create dramatic effect.

Painted in egg tempera on wood, all the colors are matte and are applied in flat areas and then modeled with white and black. The delicate, two-tone representation of skin was the result of the convention surviving from icon painting, and not abandoned until the 1450s, of underpainting with terra verde and then building up the highlights with lead white and some pink for cheeks, the latter left out when painting corpses. The greenish astringency of flesh tones contrasts pleasantly with the gold leaf's warmish tinge, a product of the bole (red earth) used to underpaint the gilded areas.

Duccio di Buoninsegna, *The Temptation of Christ on the Mountain*, 1308–1311. Tempera on wood. The gold leaf sky in the medieval tradition of icon painting was to be dropped by Italian artists of the Renaissance seeking greater realism; the conventional treatment of the architecture in pale green and pink earths was still being used by the Limbourg brothers in their *Books of Hours* almost exactly a century later. Copyright The Frick Collection, New York.

11 | Uccello

Paolo di Dono (c. 1397–1475), called Uccello for his love of birds (*uccello* means bird in Italian, and his house was reputedly full of birds and animals), painted chiefly in Florence, where he also worked for a period as a mosaicist. He is known for being obsessed with the laws of perspective and for staying up all night studying vanishing points, ignoring his wife's calls to come to bed. ". . . If only he had spent as much time on human figures and animals as he spent, and wasted, on the finer points of perspective," wrote Vasari in his *Lives of the Artists* (1550). Nevertheless, Uccello's paintings can be seen as a transition from the decorative Gothic style to the naturalism of the Renaissance.

Painted around 1460, Uccello's *St. George and the Dragon* is one of the few paintings of the time executed on canvas. It depicts the then popular tale of the marauding dragon that was on a strict diet of young women supplied by the terrified populace; when it was the King's daughter's turn to be sacrificed, St. George arrived just in time to save her, by wounding the dragon and taking it into captivity.

The studied formality of the painting is enhanced by detail as decorative as in any Flemish tapestry—flowers carpeting the ground, unnaturally puffy trees and clouds in the background, strange airforce-like markings on the dragon's wings, and above all a simple palette of gray-blue, green, gray, and white, with accents of red and a prominent coral pink (a typical motif of Uccello's). Significantly, his horse is the color of the unicorn in *The Hunt of the Unicorn* tapestries.

Though only seven years older than van Eyck, Uccello does not seem to have been much influenced by the latter's discoveries in oils. The sharpness of line implies that Uccello was still working with tempera paints (though he may have mixed in some oil to increase the saturation of some of his colors) which did not allow for successful shading and halftones. In addition, the distinctively deep and brooding olive tones of the foliage show that he was continuing the fourteenth century practice of under-painting with black instead of an opaque green as was common in the Netherlands by then.

Paolo Uccello, *Saint George and the Dragon*, c. 1460. Oil and tempera on canvas. Icon-like clarity of detail. Bright colors were becoming less important as artists concentrated increasingly on rendering perspective and painting realistic landscapes. Courtesy The National Gallery, London.

The stunning simplicity of the palette evokes the jewel-like tones of the *Très Riches Heures* that had been painted in France a half century earlier—though it is unlikely that Uccelo knew the work of the Limbourg brothers—except that the visual balance of accents against deep background colors is far more complex. Vasari again criticizes him for a tendency to use colors arbitrarily and non-naturalistically, but that is exactly their value. Uccello was using them to express a very personal vision.

12 | Piero della Francesca

While new techniques of drawing perspective brought vast stylistic changes to painting, notably a new realism, the colors used by early Renaissance artists such as Piero della Francesca (c.1420–1492), as well as Uccello, were fairly similar to those used by the anonymous weavers of the Unicorn tapestries. These luminous tones were apparently fashionable all over fifteenth-century Europe, possibly introduced by traveling Flemish painters.

Piero della Francesca, who spent most of his life living in Sansepolcro in the upper Tiber valley, was primarily influenced by Florentines such as Fra Angelico and Domenico Veneziano, but was also almost certainly aware of the work of the Flemish master Roger van der Weyden in nearby Ferrara and his rich, glowing tones and half-shadows.

Piero's greatest masterpiece is the series of frescoes of *The Legend of the True Cross* (1452–66) in Arezzo. Setting his palette apart from late-Gothic is the playing down of red and deep blue as decorative elements and the introduction of new, more complex colors, such as the three different ocher browns, the rich, relatively prominent green, and the distinctive blues. Piero's blue, here a rich turquoise but elsewhere deeply reddened, together with the pinks of the architecture and skin tones, provide the background of the frescoes and the axis of the palette. On this axis are developed simple color progressions of ochers, a deep maroon, black, white, and green, and on which, as in the Bayeux Tapestry, colors are repeated and alternated, largely in the clothing of the figures. The overall effect, in contrast to that of Gothic art, is of a picture drenched in light.

Going blind, Piero della Francesca retired in the 1480s to write theoretical treatises, including the great *De prospectiva pingendi*, on geometry and perspective. He died on October 28, 1492, the very day Christopher Columbus first set foot in the New World.

Piero della Francesca, *The Finding and Proof of the True Cross,* **1452–66. Fresco and mixed media. Arezzo, church of San Francesco, choir chapel. A complex palette of related earthtones popped by green and a rich turquoise blue. Scala/Art Resource, New York.**

13 | Jan van Eyck

Jan van Eyck (c. 1390–1441) did not invent oil painting; there are examples of linseed and walnut oils being used as paint binders from the thirteenth century on. However, he did demonstrate what could be done with oil paints in the hands of a master, and thereby changed the role of color in painting forever.

Oil reverses the way tones are built up. Where fresco and tempera painters have to use premixed colors and build up from dark to light, oil painters went from light to dark, applying layer upon layer of thin color glazes until the right dark tones are achieved. The result is enormously deep colors which, since oil stays wet for a long time, could be gently blended into each other at the edges, leading to an infinite number of intermediate tones. The downside was that many pigments used in tempera, particularly green earth, did not work well in oil. Either they were not transparent enough to make glazes, or they left a rough surface on drying, and were therefore abandoned. Many oil painters did not seem to mind.

Van Eyck was a master of tonal gradation. From the skin tones—basically the white of the primed wood with a pink glaze—to the rich deep colors of the fabrics, he had an uncanny ability to capture the way light and shadow play on a surface. Another feature of oil painting also helped in its naturalism: In tempera, the darkest colors which have to be in the first layer also have to be the most saturated; in oil, since the colors are being slowly built up on a white base, the most saturated colors appear in the midtones, right where we see them in the actual world.

Because of his skill at realism, van Eyck was in great demand as a portraitist. His major patron, Philip the Good, Duke of Burgundy, even sent him to Portugal to paint the portrait of the woman he was negotiating to marry. Philip was lucky: In many such arranged political marriages the suitor never knew what his wife really looked like until the wedding day. Unfortunately, this picture has not survived.

The Arnolfini Marriage is a similar commission for a wealthy merchant family of the Netherlands. Van Eyck is painting light. The soft northern light comes in from a window just in front of the picture plane, catching the white faces and making them the center of attention. Everything is carefully balanced: the black hat against the white veil, the red nuptial bed against the green (representing fidelity and fertility) of the dress, the touch of blue on the dress sleeves against the oranges on the table.

The way van Eyck divides the painting into two halves, one somber and brown, the other bright and colorful, indicates the rising importance of moodier, monochromatic color schemes (see Leonardo da Vinci on next page) and the increasing marginalization of brights—the latter now seeming almost effeminate.

Jan van Eyck, *The Arnolfini Marriage*, 1434. Oil on wood. An almost hyperrealist study of a fifteenth century Dutch interior, detailed down to a glimpse of an oriental pile rug which, with the red damask and some stained glass in the window, was one of the few sources of color in an austere environment. **Courtesy The National Gallery, London.**

14 | Leonardo da Vinci

Leonardo da Vinci (1452–1519) took van Eyck's developments in oil painting and color to their logical conclusion. Teaching himself anatomy, minutely observing the different ways fabrics drape, his drawings and paintings are virtuoso studies of light and shadow—chiaroscuro, as the Italians called it.

As a result, bright colors were not of primary concern to him; nor was he interested in using them as an expressive force. In fact, Leonardo developed his own method of modeling all the forms in his pictures with monochrome browns, blacks, and grays—tones that generally dominated the finished painting—before the application of any strong color.

When Leonardo used bright color it was grudgingly. He barely paid lip service to the stipulation in the contract for *The Virgin of the Rocks* (c. 1508) to use "fine colors." As was appropriate, he used blue for the Virgin Mary's dress, but he seems to have consciously darkened it. Tests of the pigments used have shown that the azurite underlayer (it was common practice in oil by then to build up a color first with an inexpensive pigment) has a definite green tinge and the purplish ultramarine covering it is layered in the thinnest possible wash, giving an overall gray effect. Similarly, the lining of the dress is a dull ocher with only a hint of yellow lake to lighten it. Only the small patches of the sea and the rocks glimpsed in the background have a layer of white lead underneath to brighten the colors.

While the large part of the painting is a mélange of warm browns with a robust black, the effect is like that of van Eyck's *Arnolfini Marriage* with its carefully balanced harmony of contrasts: again white against black, blue and blue-green against pink and brown, all orchestrated to focus attention on the four faces carefully arranged in a spiral beginning with the infant John the Baptist on the left and culminating in the infant Jesus' raised fingers and Mary's floating hand. Mathematical organization, not color, is now the symbol of God's presence in the world.

Leonardo da Vinci, *The Virgin of the Rocks*, c. 1508. Oil on wood. While his contract called for using "fine (i.e. expensive) colors" normally expected in an altarpiece like this, Leonardo preferred to explore form and space in base paints, much like the Cubists four hundred years later. Courtesy The National Gallery, London.

ANNO. 1532.   ÆTATIS. SVÆ. 29.

15 | Hans Holbein

Hans Holbein the Younger (1497/98–1543), born in Augsburg, Germany, and trained in the studio of his father, had become the leading portraitist in Basel, Switzerland, by his twenties and by 1536 was appointed court painter to King Henry VIII in London.

Holbein was the outstanding realist and colorist of the northern Renaissance. The subjects of his portraits, such as this member of the Wedigh family, have a penetrating stare that is all the more striking given the formality of the composition. Painted in 1532, this portrait is executed in both tempera (used for the blue background, as the uneven color indicates) and oil on wood. It is typical of Holbein's attention to light, to textures, whether drapery or book leaves, and to simple yet elegant color massing.

There is almost mathematical balance here, particularly in the use of color contrasts. The two sets of harmonies—light/dark, warm/cool—are perfectly controlled with two spots of yellow (on the robe lining and the book) counterbalancing the brilliant cerulean blue of the background. The same is true of the flesh pinks contrasting with the green tablecloth and the whites against the black.

For decorators of surfaces and for interior designers, Holbein offers the sensuous delight of fully saturated hues and rich tonal ranges. This is Leonardo's *Virgin of the Rocks* (see previous page) in reverse, with the accents of blue and green enlarged to take full advantage of their luscious tones in framing the central figure. Holbein also demonstrates how blue can be used to suggest an almost infinite depth of abstract space behind the sitter's head—then deliberately undermines this effect by adding lettering across it, creating complexity of perspective.

Hans Holbein the Younger, *Portrait of a Member of the Wedigh Family*, 1532. Tempera and oil on wood. Perfect control and balance with contrasting hues and tones—orange against blue, pink against green, white against black. The Metropolitan Museum of Art, Bequest of Edward S. Harkness, 1950. (50.135.4) © 1993 by The Metropolitan Museum of Art

16 | Agnolo Bronzino

The Italian sixteenth-century painter Agnolo Bronzino (1503–1562) has a reputation as the leading Florentine portraitist of the Renaissance. Court painter to the ruling Medici family, Bronzino's legacy is one of exquisitely colored images of a particularly artistic, literary, and elegant society.

Bronzino was a mannerist, favoring elongated and delicate forms and full chromatic statements. His palette focused on cool blacks, blues, and greens, porcelain-like flesh tones, and at times a rich but still cool pink. The Renaissance art historian Giorgio Vasari (1511–1574), who wrote in praise of maniera, claimed that Bronzino and other mannerists "attained to the greatest beauty from the practice which arose of constantly copying the most beautiful objects and joining these together with the most beautiful hands, heads, bodies and legs so as to make a figure of the greatest possible beauty to see."

In his psychologically penetrating portrait of Lodovico Capponi, Bronzino confines his palette to a range of radiant pinks and vibrant whites and blacks set against his favorite muted tone of green. Harmony is based on the simple contrasts of pink with green and black with white, all carefully focusing attention on the light-bathed face and hands. The simplicity of the color scheme accentuates the importance given to the play of light and shade in rendering the folds of drapery and costume; now that they were virtuosos in techniques of chiaroscuro, artists no longer seemed interested in using expensive pigments such as ultramarine and gold to suggest wealth (although blue does figure in other Bronzino paintings). The high finish and depth of color achieved by the use of oil paint built up in thin glazes adds to the painting's refinement.

Even with the wired color sensibility of the late-twentieth century, the bold, at times harsh, schemes of mannerists like Bronzino, as well as El Greco (see page 34), still intrigue by virtue of the exaggerated strength of color statements. As such, the mannerist palettes are best employed when the desired end result is drama and mood, such as in advertising and theater design.

Agnolo Bronzino, *Lodovico Capponi*, c. 1550–55. Oil on wood. Portrait of a page at the Medici court in Florence, wearing his family's armorial colors of black and white. Copyright The Frick Collection, New York.

17 | El Greco

Domenicos Theotocopoulos, known as El Greco (1541–1614), "the Greek," was born on Crete, worked in Venice and Rome, and finally settled in Toledo, Spain, c. 1575. His paintings display all the subjective, exaggerated, sometimes acidly colored emotionalism for which Mannerism is known; they have the drama and metaphysical presence, worked out in strong color, of earlier icons (he actually trained first as an icon painter), and his flame-like line accentuated by vivid highlights perfectly complements his distorted and wracked figures.

The Expulsion from the Temple (1604) blows the prim classicism of Leonardo out of the water. It is all movement and power as Christ physically drives out the merchants from the sanctuary, their harshly colored robes popping out vividly against the subtle color-cast neutrals of the skin tones and background architecture. Even the adhesive fleshiness of the impasto, the heavy brushstrokes, and the raw areas where the canvas shows through give the impression that the artist has attacked his task with real anger, lacking the patience to build up color with glaze upon glaze.

Yet there is method to El Greco's madness. Even as the left side of the painting seems to collapse, the figures knocked off balance by a swing of Christ's arm while those on the right seem to wait nervously for their turn, the whole is united through the strong color blocking. Not only the open arch, which frames his head like a halo, with its peaceful blue sky beyond promising salvation, but also the swirling yellows and greens focus the eye in on the central figure dressed in red—red, as in the old icon tradition, for the blood of Christ, not a warm carmine but the cool, anguished, purplish red (madder lake tinted with ultramarine blue) that is El Greco's hallmark.

This is a dazzling display of color and texture. The phosphorescent qualities of all the acidified reds, yellows, and blues, together with an eerie chartreuse, suggest the otherworldly. El Greco is a narrator who tells stories with the color he paints, and by electing color over line as a unifying agent, he was a true modernist.

El Greco, *Purification of the Temple*, c. 1600.
Oil on canvas. Dramatic effects from cold but
intense colors heighten the anger shown by Christ
as he drives out the moneychangers from the
temple precincts. Copyright The Frick Collection,
New York.

Colors of historic European and American interiors. With hardwoods such as oak (needed for traditional paneling) becoming increasingly rare and expensive in seventeenth-century Europe, paints came into use to disguise the new softwoods such as deal and fir. American colonists, who from the first were often dependent on such wood, were quick to follow the fashions of the Old World.

18 | The Dutch Home—Through Vermeer's Eyes

A novel feature of Jan Vermeer's (1632–1675) paintings is that almost all of his surviving thirty paintings represent women—not women as Madonnas or saints but as ordinary people in ordinary household settings, engaged in intimate and personal activities. This was no peculiarity of his taste. In fact, the Dutch invented the concept of the house as a private place for the family alone, and paintings of home interiors became enormously popular amongst the bourgeois middle class of seventeenth century Netherlands, a tiny country experiencing an enormous economic boom through manufacturing and trade much as Japan did in the 1980s.

Revealing in all such paintings of the period is the austerity and cleanliness of the interiors. Furniture was limited to the minimum number of tables, chairs, and beds, together with an oriental carpet draped over the table, curtains (a Dutch invention), and the occasional musical instrument. This minimalism was partly due to the puritan Calvinist religion—favorite clothing colors were dark: black, violet, or brown, though women also favored blue (shown here) and butter yellow—and partly because women, even at the highest levels of society, did their own housework, so it was in their best interests to have a simple, easy-to-clean home.

Vermeer's subdued palette captures the simplicity of the Dutch interior, from the black-and-white inlaid floor and the plain whitewashed walls to the unpainted ceilings, and it allows him to concentrate on the effects of light pouring in through the oversize windows (another Dutch innovation). The snapshot-like, almost voyeuristic style is probably influenced by the camera obscura, a popular toy of the time that allowed one to project an image onto a screen. Vermeer's paintings use the same contrasts of in-focus and out-of-focus details and disjunction of tones that the instrument would produce.

The Lady's Secrets

Vermeer provides a lesson in the use of color as an accent, for he uses flat areas of stronger hues against the predominant cool neutrals to focus attention on certain details. The most popular accent is yellow, usually worn by his female figures but here seen only in the gilt frame of the hanging picture, followed by a warm red, here only in the ribbons on her sleeves, and a blue that in other paintings varies to a rich topaz blue or even a jade green. The jewel-like colors that are almost a little too rich are coloristic references to the limpid tones and resplendent nudes of the Renaissance masters. They

also help convey the undercurrent of eroticism, alluded to by love letters and pictures of cupid hanging on the wall, that runs throughout Vermeer's paintings, allowing us a glimpse of another side of the Dutch lady left to her own devices for long stretches of time by her seafaring husband.

Vermeer, *A Young Woman Standing at a Virginal*, c. 1660s. Light and air suffuse this painting of a woman entertaining an unseen visitor. In an allusion to chastity and the Virgin Mary, the figure wears a blue blouse; a favorite Dutch color influenced by imported Ming porcelain from China, the blue is picked up in the three hanging paintings, the chair upholstery, and the Delft tiles running around the base of the wall. **Courtesy The National Gallery, London.**

I have seen but one idea in all the houses here, the rooms are white and gold...
[I] could perceive no difference but in more or less gold...
—Horace Walpole, letter to Anne Pitt, December 25, 1765

19 | Rococo's Glitzy Interiors

Rococo was the first architectural style developed essentially for interiors only. Unlike baroque forms, the swirls and scrolls of rococo ornamentation were rarely used on exteriors, and the room decors largely reflected the influence of a newly preeminent group in French social and cultural life—women. It was the women at the courts of Louis XIV (1638–1715) and his great grandson Louis XV (1710–1774) such as Mme de Maintenon and Mme de Pompadour, who popularized this lighter style with its new sense of intimacy, in which the rooms are decorated with carved paneling, matching furniture, and integrated tapestries and carpets in the earliest examples of fully coordinated design.

Rococo is a nineteenth-century semantic marriage of baroque (*barocco* in Italian) and *rocaille* (French for rockwork), an appropriate name since the inspiration for the ornamentation came from the curved, sinuous lines of waves, pouring water and seashells, also the source of the eighteenth century's predominant color—white. Walpole's gold was the gilding used to highlight the carving on wall panels and on furniture, further accentuated by flickering candlelight from fixtures mounted right against the wall. To be fair to the

French, even wealthy homeowners could only afford gold in their most important reception rooms, which may have been all Walpole saw. The effect of light-filled interiors was heightened by the new fashion for incorporating large mirrors into the paneling, often in place of paintings or tapestries.

Rococo scrollwork against a ground of gray-green. The effect of the gilded carving would be further enhanced by flickering candlelight from brackets mounted against the walls. Courtesy Theo Crosby, London.

Where color was used it was comparatively restrained, with a preference for the tones of natural materials, particularly marble, real or faux, or the delicate shades of Boucher's designs for the Gobelins' tapestries. Other color came from fabrics mounted on the walls, imported Chinese wallpapers—cheaper than the French equivalents—and paint, notably yellow and celadon green; these colors were relatively strong at the start of the eighteenth century, but became extremely pale during Louis XV's reign, again to maximize the amount of available light. Brighter color was reserved for upholstery (often crimson) on the newly padded furniture, and most strikingly for the porcelain that was an important decorative accent.

Pompadour Rose

Louis XV's famous mistress, Mme de Pompadour, one of the period's most important patrons of design, helped promote the search for a French porcelain in 1738, establishing a porcelain factory in 1748 in the palace at Vincennes, and moving it to Sèvres near one of her homes in 1753. Her patronage was recognized by having one of the most striking colors of the palette named after her. The palette was apparently influenced by Pompadour's own extensive collection of Chinese decorative art, but Sèvres colors are distinctive in their own right. Most were developed by chemist Jean Hellot, who had begun his career improving dyes for the tapestry works and was responsible for the purple-blue (*bleu lapis,* 1753, replaced by the navy *bleu nouveau* in 1763), the famous turquoise (*bleu céleste,* also 1753), green (*vert,* 1756) and pink (*Pompadour rose,* 1757). Yellow and violet appeared briefly as well, but both were dropped for technical or commercial reasons.

As in interiors, gold was used as trim for the designs and the ground colors, where it helped hide unevenness at the edges, and from the early nineteenth century on itself appeared as a ground color. Gold, however, was only a small part of the huge cost of Sèvres porcelain, of which typically only five percent came out perfectly after firing and burnishing. An order from Louis XVI in 1783 for a 445-piece dinner set specified that it be delivered within twenty years and cost no more than 480 pounds apiece; that order was cut short by Louis's execution in 1793, but the factory still exists to this day.

20 | Adam Brothers' Classicism

Robert and James Adam, the most successful members of a lowland Scots family of contractor-architects, were responsible for moving British interior design of the eighteenth century toward a lighter, sparser classical style that has come to be named after them.

As was the tradition at the time, each brother spent several years on a grand tour of Italy and closely studied surviving Etruscan and Roman buildings. The elder brother, Robert Adam (1728–92), settled in London in 1758, where he was joined by James (1732–94) in 1762. Cultivating an aristocratic clientele, they were soon commissioned to build, or more often to renovate, many important country houses and London town residences including Syon House (1762–9) and Osterley Park (1761–80).

Central to the Adam style was the use of color. In their seminal book, *Works in Architecture*, published in 1773, they described how they used "light tints of pink and green ... to relieve the ornaments [and to] remove the crudeness of white," the allover white that had characterized the rococo style. By banishing bold effects of relief and mass in favor of more delicate plasterwork, they became more dependent on painted decoration. In fact, the colors they used were far stronger than often thought, probably influenced by the striking interior schemes they had seen in Italy, some of which were modern, while others dated back to the Renaissance. None of them were strictly classical, however.

Cool and Controlled

Pink and green were central to the Adam palette through the 1760s, which together with pale blue and wheaten yellow provided simple contrasts for picking out the architectural details, particularly on the ceiling, which was one of the most important unifying elements in their interiors. While the relief plasterwork was originally gilded as in France, it was increasingly left white with washes of color providing the background. In the 1770s, the Adams shifted away from contrasts toward more complex monochromatic harmonies using multiple greens and mauves instead of pinks. Overall, there was an unusual coherence to the palette, all the colors being of a roughly even value and cool in tonality, that mirrored the architectural unity of the interiors.

The Adams followed the French example of controlling all aspects of design, from plasterwork to furniture. English craftsmen, used to working independently—often resulting in strange mélanges of taste—were now carefully trained and closely supervised so that the brothers' color sense extended to the choice of colored furnishings (often a strong cerise or crimson) that contrasted and harmonized with the interiors. The painting of wall surfaces was also carefully planned, and, since colors often had to be ground and mixed on the spot, hand-colored elevations (which still exist in the Sir John Soane Museum in London) showing not just the hue but even the exact shades, were supplied for matching by the craftsmen.

Robert Adam, *Working Drawing for Table for Lord Bathurst,* Apsley House, Piccadilly, London, c. 1770s. The soft but clear colors that the Adams featured on their ceiling were also picked up on walls and on furniture. The table shows a variety of colors repeatedly used by the brothers, notably the rose pink, pale blue, and grayish verdigris green (seen most clearly on the feet). Courtesy The Trustees of Sir John Soane's Museum, London.

I only pretend to have attempted to copy the fine antique forms, but not with absolute servility. I have endeavored to preserve the style and spirit of if you please the elegant simplicity on antique forms...

—J. Wedgwood, letter to Dr. Erasmus Darwin, 1789

21 | Wedgwood Blues

Like the Adam brothers, Wedgwood was also greatly influenced by classical styles, but while ancient Greeks avoided color in ceramics, Wedgwood reveled in it. Because of his minute attention to detail and to nuance of hue, many of his colors are stunning, and the blues—pale, medium and deep—are unique.

Josiah Wedgwood (1730–1795) was a renaissance man of the early industrial revolution. Potter, chemist, industrialist, antiquarian, he made his fortune from basaltesware (1769), a black stoneware of his own recipe which he decorated in the red-figure Attic (see Sophisticated Greek Earthtones, page 4) style. After several years of experimentation he perfected a white version of stoneware, called jasper (1775), the finest substitute for porcelain ever made and the first to successfully undercut the ware coming from China.

Cameo Role

Jasper is better known now because of its colors, which Wedgwood matched to antique cameos instead of ceramics, forging a completely new direction in tableware. He originally mixed pigment into the clay itself (solid jasper), but since blue pigments were still very expensive (the best cobalt was a strictly controlled export from Saxony), and smuggling was punishable by death, he saved money by simply staining the finished piece or by dipping in a colored slip before firing. Blue was a logistical nightmare all around: it depended on minute control of the firing temperature, which is why shades varied from a deep blue of startling vibrancy to muted, lighter tones with a greenish astringency. It was also affected by the quality of pigment available at the time, with a distinctive grayer blue being particularly associated with the Wedgwood Factory at the end of the nineteenth century.

Other shades include a famous lilac, cane yellow, brick red with a pinkish cast, pale avocado, and warm bark brown, colors favored by the burgeoning neoclassical movement and ones that, though subtly different, coordinated very successfully with the Adam interior colors. Because no glaze was used, colors are always matte and have a slightly dusty, translucent look not unlike that of a watercolor. Generally, the molded reliefs were left white, perfectly set off against the monochromatic ground.

While Wedgwood did produce some combinations, such as green with brown, the monochromatics were always the most successful designs. Nevertheless, multiple harmonies can be achieved relatively easily by the reader using this palette, since all the colors tend to be of equal value, or depth.

Cooler and more serious than pastels, the Wedgwood colors convey a sense of calm; the minimalist purity of the jasper has never become dated, and production of jasperware continues today.

Wedgwood, teaware and pitcher, c. 1785–90. Lapidary-polished jasperware with white relief. The distinctive pale colors, derived from ancient cameos, of this ware coordinated perfectly with the Adam brothers' neo-classical schemes. The single most famous product of the Wedgwood factories, Jasperware is still produced today. Courtesy Birmingham Museum of Art, Birmingham, Alabama, The Dwight and Lucille Beeson Wedgwood Collection.

22 | Colonial America's Imported Taste

The settling of America was a utopian adventure and a new beginning for many of Europe's disadvantaged, but the settlers, while escaping religious and economic oppression, in fact imported their culture with them whole and intact to this new land, making little or no reference to native American

cultures when it came to building and decorating their houses, at least until the Art Deco period.

At first, survival was at a subsistence level; interiors of the simple wooden houses were simply whitewashed with slaked lime. By the early eighteenth century, however, the success of the colonies was drawing cabinet makers, carpenters, painters, and other skilled craftsmen across the Atlantic. With them came a color sense, whether of Spanish influence in Florida, French in Louisiana, or English in much of the rest of the territories, together with their respective pigments.

The New England palette was largely deep and drab, reflecting Georgian taste in Britain. Imported colors included Prussian blue, red lead, vermilion (mercuric sulphide), and verdigris (made by exposing copper to vinegar fumes and scraping off the surface encrustation), a soft middle to deep green that was popular in England throughout the eighteenth century and has come to be known as Georgian green. These colors were often harmonized with neutral hues of similar tones including grays, putty colors, and off-whites mixed from earth pigments. In addition, a certain amount of gold and brass leaf was used to highlight details.

Earth Browns and Blood Red

While Colonial Americans were heavily dependent on imported blocks of dried pigments, outside the cities, most farmers and rural businessmen could not afford these fancy colors and instead employed the skills of traveling painters to find and grind colors from local earths, plants, berries, or even dried animal blood.

As a result, the country palette evolved into a characteristic range of warm and somber colors such as a range of ochers from pale pink to dark red and a brighter cane yellow, together with some copper greens. Given the unavailability of even linseed oil in remote places, many of the pigments were mixed with buttermilk, a residue of the butter-making process, which on drying gave a distinctive matte surface. Even white lead paint was beyond the means of most and, in general, color was restricted to the woodwork, and walls above the wainscoting were still whitewashed.

The Library, Brush-Everard House, Williamsburg, c. 1770. A colonial-era interior showing a particularly intense copper-based green. Characteristic of the period, the wood paneling and trim is painted in a deep color, while the wall itself is whitewashed. Courtesy Colonial Williamsburg Foundation.

23 | **Federal America: Fashion Victim**

The history of American color use is one of considerable overlap—colors used in the early seventeenth century, such as gray-greens and dull pinks, were still being used into the nineteenth century, although largely only in rural areas.

European fashions, glimpsed in pattern books published in London, continued to drive American color taste in urban centers such as Boston and New York following the independence of the colonies. Important pigments coming over included the perennial favorite Prussian blue and the new strong yellows such as Turner's yellow (not named for the painter, but a London paint manufacturer). The Adam brothers made the use of brighter and clearer colors respectable, ultimately supplanting the softer Williamsburg colors (themselves influenced by Sir Christopher Wren), although white-painted paneling was becoming increasingly popular. In fact, the Colonial and Federal periods can roughly be distinguished by the taste for colored paneling and whitewashed walls in the former, and colored walls with white paneling in the latter.

The growing wealth of the American middle classes also meant that quantities of Turkish and Persian carpets were beginning to arrive, with their earthy reds and indigo blues sometimes picked up in trim and upholstery in perfect complement to the yellow-painted rooms.

Washington's Weakness

Detailed analysis of pigments used at historic buildings such as the Mount Vernon home of George Washington (1732–1799), show just how remarkably bright the original colors were. The pale greens, blues, and grays that have been considered authentic for the past hundred years have been replaced by the vibrant greens (in both light, as shown here, and dark tones) and Prussian blues that Washington enjoyed in the 1790s, sometimes with a solid black dado or baseboard in the Pompeiian style. However, given the considerable expense of the pigments, in his and most interiors of the period, the brightest colors were reserved for the more public areas, such as drawing rooms, dining rooms, and guest bedrooms. For private rooms such as studies and master bedrooms, pale but warm shades of earth-pigmented buff and brown, as well as plain whitewash, were acceptable.

Prussian blue was probably the most expensive pigment to be had, but Washington used it lavishly in at least two rooms at Mount Vernon—the downstairs bedroom and the front parlor. It had the curious quality of appearing darker the more pressure was applied with the brush, giving it the

irregular or striated appearance seen here. The other important color in the restoration is the definitely bluish verdigris green used in the dining rooms and for some trim. The simple pine paneling in the hallway was also painted in a rich brown and grained to simulate more expensive woods. The strong yellow was a favorite at the time on both sides of the Atlantic (it was used strikingly at Jefferson's house, Monticello), and was often complemented by curtains or drapery in the yellow-green or deep red shown on the palette.

By 1820, as Greek revival was reaching its peak, color had been largely eliminated from walls and trim, replaced by all-pervasive white or by flat yellow, roughly simulating marble, both inside and out, with only exterior shutters in deep bottle and chrome greens in emulation of the stunning bronze shutters of Renaissance buildings. The notable exception was carpets, which, now being manufactured in the United States, increasingly used larger patterns and added a brilliant pink to the existing blue and yellow.

South wall of Large Dining Room, Mount Vernon, Virginia, c. 1799. The two shades of verdigris green are documented as the original colors; the trim and molding is painted, on Washington's instructions, "a buff inclining to white"; the doors have an artificial mahogany finish. The new Federal style is heavily influenced by the Adam Brothers designs in England. Courtesy Mount Vernon Ladies Association.

After the French Revolution of 1789 and the execution of Louis XVI, a new style blossomed in Paris of the 1790s, quickly replacing the discredited rococo of the *ancien régime*. This style was to become closely associated with Napoleon's empire from 1804 to his defeat at Waterloo in 1815, but remained popular in Europe and America for years after.

The Empire Style was created by two Parisian interior decorators, Charles Percier (1764–1838) and his business partner Pierre-François-Léonard Fontaine (1762–1853), after their return from studying classical and Renaissance architecture in Italy in 1791. The style took off when the pair was commissioned by Joséphine Bonaparte to redecorate her home Malmaison in 1799 after an introduction by the Romantic painter Jacques-Louis David. They were subsequently taken on by Napoleon to design an appropriate visual background to his grandiose activities.

Though stagy and lavishly decorated with antique motifs, their furnishings and fittings are not in themselves remarkable; it was their color schemes that sent a shock wave through post-revolutionary Parisian society. The illusionistic scenic wallpaintings and faux marbling and graining of the previous decades were swept away by the sparse decorations but exciting colors of the Grecian or Pompeiian taste that both designers had seen in the excavations of Pompeii and Herculaneum. Interiors were now decorated with extensive areas of strong, flat color usually unpatterned and featuring a bold border.

Romanticism

The original colors that can be seen in drawings for Mme Récamier's private rooms present delicate, feminine, and enormously complex harmonies of pale pastels—including the distinctive grayed blues and violets, together with apricot, cream, and an accent of black—that prefigure the soft palettes of art nouveau interiors almost exactly a century later. For Napoleon's pro-pagandistic purposes, the palette was deepened and enriched with strongly contrasting tones of purple (once again an imperial color), brilliant lemon yellow, and deep apple green, complemented by strong pink or red and often set off against white grounds and gold motifs.

Key to the interiors is a voluptuous use of fabrics, with satin particularly favored for drapery and dyed in brilliant green, rich purple, and crimson or brilliant yellow. White fabrics were also introduced as drapes to set off these colors, though often more as an accent than as a background; perhaps white was a symbol of purity within this sensuous profusion of color. A new feature of Empire interiors were the "tent" rooms with all walls and ceiling hung with pleated fabric. These had been previously installed by men of military background, but were now available to both sexes. Their theatrical intimacy suggested more romantic notions of Turkey and the East than military encampments.

Robert Smirke, Mme Récamier's bedroom, 1802. Watercolor sketch. Decorated in 1798 by L. M. Berthault, probably helped by Percier, the bedroom is a classic example of the rage for Pompeiian ornamentation and soft colorations then sweeping Paris. The violet silk wall hangings have a printed black border, and the buff-colored silk pelmet has a gold border. Courtesy British Architectural Library, RIBA, London.

25 | **Victorian Overstuffed Interiors**

The defining feature of the Victorian interior throughout much of the middle and late nineteenth century was the sheer eclecticism of styles used, and often mixed, for interior decoration, drawing from historical sources as disparate as French baroque and rococo, as well as Pompeiian, Grecian, Empire, and even Turkish and Egyptian. Jakob von Falke observed at the 1876 International Exhibition in Vienna that "the modern Frenchman dwells in the eighteenth century, he sleeps in that century likewise, but he dines in the sixteenth, then on occasion he smokes his cigar and enjoys his coffee in the Orient, while he takes his bath in Pompeii . . ."

Particularly influential were several books published on historic colors including Jakob-Ignatius Hittorff's treatise on the painting of classical temples in *L'Architecture Polychrome chez les Grecs* (1851), Owen Jones's *The Grammar of Ornament* (1856) and Charles Eastlake's *A History of the*

Gothic Revival (1872), all of which stimulated an interest in polychromy which extended from the fading out of Empire soft lavenders and pinks around 1850 well into the 1890s.

The profusion of colors—many of those shown here would have been used simultaneously—were harmonized by the simple expedient of darkening them until they all became relatively easily balanced tones, much like in the Turkish carpets that had now become quite commonplace in upper and middle class interiors. Even the newly invented synthetic dyes and pigments such as aniline purple, alizarin crimson (a color which still carried connotations of grandeur and was frequently used on walls in the form of flock wallpaper), and chromium oxide green did not escape this treatment.

Warmth and Comfort

This new taste for somber schemes, replacing the light and airy colors of Georgian rooms, may have been sparked by architectural concerns. High ceilings had become a fashion that was to last until the Arts and Crafts Movement, and architects like Frank Lloyd Wright brought in low ceilings at the end of the century. Apart from problems heating them, Victorians evidently thought white made these rooms seem excessively high and chilling. Around the late 1830s, it became common to tint the ceilings again and to paint the cornices in even darker shades. Interiors were made to seem warmer and cosier by bringing the color schemes down onto the walls as well, and thick, heavy curtains and even stained glass helped cut down the light coming in—a style encouraged by William Morris, who thought "modern" windows much too large.

Again, as we have seen in many of the examples chosen here of interiors, women played a significant part in the story. Finally acknowledging their role, new books full of domestic detail and design advice aimed directly at women started to appear in the mid-nineteenth century. These included *A Treatise on Domestic Economy for Young Ladies* (1841) by Catherine Beecher (sister of Harriet Beecher Stowe) and von Falke's *Art in the House* (1871) which devoted a chapter to "woman's aesthetic mission." These books undermined the philosophy of austerity that determined Georgian taste and instead advocated functional and easily maintained interiors, loosely arranged furniture, and comfortable, as well as presumably dirt-hiding, colors.

Eastman Johnson, *The Hatch Family*, 1871. Oil on canvas. A detailed record of the mid-Victorian preference for warm but drab colors and heavy drapery. Note the brilliant green dress worn by the seated girl on the right, colored with the new synthetic dyes. Courtesy The Metropolitan Museum of Art, New York, Gift of Frederic H. Hatch, 1926. (26.97) © 1983 by The Metropolitan Museum of Art

Orientalism

Palettes inspired by the Far East. With fine Chinese porcelain, Persian carpets, and Indian fabrics streaming in from as early as the fourteenth century, Europeans, and later Americans, were endlessly fascinated by the exotic colors and designs, particularly in the eighteenth and nineteenth centuries.

26 | Moorish Spain's Tiles

The technique of tin-glazing earthenware came to Europe in the eleventh century through Spain, the furthest outpost of Islamic power. Tin glaze, developed in imitation of Chinese porcelain, provides an opaque white ground with a bluish tint that sets off other colors beautifully; it was to become the basis of the *majolica* industry. In the thirteenth century, the introduction of cobalt blue, also from the Middle East, further revolutionized European ceramics.

This particular palette appears in tilework of southern Spain, Portugal, Tunisia, and Morocco, but most spectacularly in the Alhambra, the "red castle," Granada's fortress-palace built by the Nasrid kings from 1248 to 1354. The building is a remarkable confection of hanging stucco ornament dramatically energized by multicolor dadoes in an inspired, sophisticated scheme of black, limpid emerald green, gray-blue, orangey terra-cotta, and buff (from copper, cobalt, and antimony), which has precedents in Egyptian wall painting.

Originally, as Owen Jones observed in his pioneering study, *Plans, Elevations, Sections and Details of the Alhambra* (1836), the stucco, though mostly bare today, was also brightly colored to complement the tiles: "On moulded surfaces they placed red, the strongest [primary], in the depths, where it would be softened by shadow, never on the surface; blue in the shade, and gold on all surfaces exposed to light … The several colors are either separated by white bands, or by the shadow caused by the relief of the ornament itself—and this appears to be an absolute principle required in colouring—*colours should never be allowed to impinge on each other.*"

Isolating Colors

To isolate visually the colors on the tiles and prevent the glazes from running together in the kiln and spoiling the geometric effect, any one of three methods was used in southern Spain: in *cuerda seca* (dry cord) the glazes were separated by string impregnated with grease, which burned off in the kiln, leaving brown or black lines; in *cuenca*, the geometric patterns were stamped into the clay and the depressions filled with the appropriate glaze now separated from its neighbor by a small ridge; or, as in the Alhambra, a mosaic could simply be built up using tiles glazed flat with a single color.

Green and the blue are symbolically important Muslim colors, referring respectively to the color of the prophet Mohammed's robe and, in parched desert regions, to heaven. Note the close relationship of these two colors:

hardly distinguishable at any distance, their interplay neatly subverts any tendency of the design to be too cut-and-dried. Terra-cotta, cream, and black were the prototypical colors of the lead-glazed tiles found all over medieval Europe. So this palette, which was to

Cuenca tile in the Moorish style, c. 1890. An accurate reproduction of the original tiles used in southern Spain and North Africa, from Caldes da Rainha, Portugal. The four individual tiles interlock into a complicated geometric pattern that could be spread across a wall. Courtesy Solar Antique Tiles, New York.

evolve into the majolica style (see next page), represents the meeting of two cultures, Islamic and Christian, on the Iberian peninsular.

Inevitably, the arts have returned to this scheme to explore the two sides of Spain's national character. Barcelona's famous architect, Antonio Gaudí, was the first to appreciate the importance of Spain's Islamic past, and he minutely matched Moorish schemes in his tiled art nouveau masterpieces such as the Palacio Guell. A similar blue-buff-black palette was the recurring favorite of Spanish-born artists such as Picasso and the Surrealists Miró and Dali.

Renaissance Italy's Majolica

In thirteenth to fifteenth century Italy, *majolica* was a generic term for all tin-glazed earthenware and metallicized luster ware imported from Moorish Spain via the island of Majorca, from which it got its name. Enormously popular both as tableware and even for insetting into the facades of buildings, majolica was copied by local potters, though with only limited success at first. For, while they had the technology for the distinctive opaque white tin glaze that provided the ground, they could not reproduce the luster glazes until the sixteenth century.

Original Italian ware had simple designs consisting of a pattern cut through white slip to the red clay underneath and reinforced by blotches of green and honey-brown glaze. Gradually, from around 1420, the incising was replaced by drawn designs and painted scenes. By the 1480s, a rich palette had been achieved which supplemented the basic copper green and manganese purple-brown with two new colors, cobalt blue and antimony yellow or orange (used in imitation of the Islamic gold and coppery lusters). Olive green could also be produced from antimony and soda, and mauve purple from manganese mixed with cobalt.

Color Out of Fire

As well as an enlarged palette, Italian majolica benefited from a major technical development—"flat painting." After dipping a piece into or pouring on a white tin glaze, painters applied the ground up and diluted metallic oxides with brushes directly onto the dried glaze before firing. Able to achieve a basic level of shading, painters could produce figurative drawings, usually of historical or mythological subjects as in the *istoriato* style. When applied, the oxides were dirty shades of grays and browns, and only after firing did they acquire their brilliant tones, thus contributing to a sense that color, produced by an almost alchemic transformation through fire in the kiln, possessed magical and mysterious qualities.

Because majolica dispensed with complicated and labor-intensive techniques used in Moorish ceramics such as *cuerda seca* and *cuenca*, pieces could be easily mass-produced. The outline of the image was "pounced" onto the surface with charcoal through a paper pattern with holes pricked in it. Designs could be supplied by artists so all the pottery painter had to do was trace the outline, fill in the colors, and add some decorative details of his own so that the pieces were not too similar.

The style soon spread across Europe up to Holland in the north and Portugal in the west (where the tradition remained strong for centuries), becoming particularly common in floor tiles, although the glazed surface did not stand up to wear very well. Some artists, such as the Della Robbia family, took the technique in a sculptural direction. Luca della Robbia (c. 1399–1482), apparently impressed with the new colors and the possibilities of working in clay, turned from carving marble to making his distinctive plaques and relief sculptures. Capitalizing on the strong white of the tin glaze, he and his followers used color largely for backgrounds, ornamental details, and occasionally clothing. The colors remained the basic cobalt blue, copper green, manganese purple, and antimony yellow, and are often the only surviving touch of color on austere Renaissance exteriors.

Pieter Frans von Venedigen, majolica tile portrait of an unknown elder, 1532. Part of a tile pavement made in Flanders for the Abbey of Herckenrode. This "medallion" was one of many with different figures interspersed with trapezoidal tiles with plant motifs in a simplified form of the tesselation used in Islamic tiling. Again, the colors are the same as in Italian and Portuguese majolica. Courtesy Solar Antique Tiles, New York.

28 | Turkey's Iznik Tiles

Like almost all blue-and-white ceramics, Iznik ware first appeared as a substitute for the costly Ming porcelain coming from China. However, as new colors were added, the potters of this little town seventy miles southwest of Istanbul acquired an international reputation of their own.

Originally using only cobalt blue for patterns (c. 1490–1520), Iznik potters matured gradually, first adding a turquoise and then, in a flash of innovation in the 1530s, perfectly subtle copper greens never before used, starting as a leaf green and soon evolving into the characteristic pistachio green. By the 1540s, they were incorporating a reddish purple, developed from manganese, a very difficult glaze to control, into their tableware. Color boundaries were kept crisp by the cuerda seca process.

The breakthrough for the potters of this small industrial town came around 1552, when the Ottoman sultan Suleyman the Magnificent (1494–1566) placed vast orders for ceramic tiles to decorate palaces and mosques across his empire. Protective, single-color glazed facades on buildings are relatively common across the Middle East, dating back to the Babylonian and Assyrian cultures of the third millenium BC. Before and during the rise of the Ottoman Empire, a range of designs, including zoomorphic, floral, and geometric motifs, supplemented monochrome tiling, generally in light and dark blue, the intense purple modena, turquoise, and gold, the last produced in a luster technique still not fully understood. These pigments were underpainted beneath a transparent blue-tint glaze and fired at high temperature, after which black, brown, and white were overpainted for another low-temperature firing.

Colors that Fade at a Distance

The main drawback of this palette for architectural applications was that, seen at a distance, purple tended to fade into the blue background. The contribution of the Iznik potters, who used the same glazing techniques, was the discovery of a much stronger red in Armenian bole, an iron-rich earth containing a trace of uranium. This was known as "sealing-wax" red because it always appeared a little in relief, as the glaze application had to be particularly thick. Used moderately at first, as in the Sulemaniye Mosque in Istanbul, this red became superabundant during the second half of the sixteenth and first twenty years of the seventeenth centuries. Unfortunately, though the potters managed to eliminate yellow and gold from the tile palette, they had to replace the subtle pistachio and sage greens with a much brighter emerald green, more suitable for architecture.

Always set against the slightly off-white ground, this palette is a fine example of warm red balancing a deep blue, one of the most powerful combinations available (and, coincidentally, later to be a favorite for the national flags of the Christian West). Distinctive to this application, however, is the minty green, which adds dimensionality and relieves the potential oppressiveness of red, white, and blue. Turquoise is a good substitute for green, and pale lavender can be added for a four-color scheme.

Iznik architectural tile, c. 1590. Showing the strong red that the Iznik potters were the first to achieve using Armenian bole, a ferruginous earth containing just a trace of uranium. Copyright British Museum.

The Mughals, who seized much of northern India in 1526, were a branch of the Mongol Timurid dynasties that conquered Persia in 1369. Both are renowned for extraordinary, often colorful, architecture—from Tamerlane's (1336–1405) turquoise tile-encrusted mausoleum in his arid capital of Samarkand to the almost translucent white marble of Shah Jehan's (1592–1666) tomb, the Taj Mahal, in verdant Agra. But the fuller record of prevailing color taste can be found in painted miniatures safely locked up for centuries inside bound books.

Timurid miniatures from Shiraz (now in Iran) and Herat (now in Afghanistan) display unequalled liveliness of color in landscapes full of figures and action, with particular shades of red, orange, and pale mint green being favored. These last two colors were apparently imported when Tamerlane's great grandson, Babur, invaded India, complementing and effectively revolutionizing the staid grayed blues, yellows, reds, and dark greens that characterized native Indian painting. The resulting palette is an unusually successful balance of jewel-like brights with earthy neutrals.

Visitors from around the World

The Mughal miniatures tended toward simpler arrangements of brightly dressed figures against plain (often mint green) backgrounds or set in wonderful, seemingly Chinese-inspired, landscapes. Most striking are the portraits of important court figures or visiting functionaries standing in a fairly natural profile pose and often in orange robes. These likenesses were kept in albums as if in a photo library and used to supply tracings for inclusion in other paintings, such as group scenes. The Mughal emperors were also keen collectors of information on the natural world: Shah Jehan's father Jehangir collected thousands of botanical drawings of flowers, which were again reproduced as decorative motifs on the gilded borders of other drawings, and would send artists to Goa, the Portuguese trading colony, to paint the exotic animals arriving from around the world. His favorite artist Masur captured a striking likeness of the then exotic turkey.

Mughal contact with European civilization through Goa also extended to copying Western paintings. The resulting influence on the Mughal palette was slight, but they did start to incorporate some tricks of perspective, including a bluing of colors at the horizon to give a sense of depth. One bizarre touch was the introduction of faint halos around the heads in Mughal portraits; the artists evidently appreciated the visual effect without intending the symbolic connotation.

Akbar Lost and Found Again, c. 1600–1620. Victoria and Albert Museum, London.
Gouache on paper. Delicate tints of the landscape provide the background for the
rich colors of the hunting party's clothing. Scala/Art Resource, New York.

It is unlikely that Vermeer knew about the origins of the designs on tapestry-weave kilims, the precursors of the knotted Persian carpets that his countrymen introduced into Western Europe, but if he had, he would probably have been amused by their relevance to his own discreet themes of sexuality (see The Dutch Home, page 36). For shreds of archaeological evidence suggest that many motifs used on kilims date back seven thousand years to early fertility cults.

Among the oldest wovens known, kilims have always been the leading art form of nomadic societies of the Middle East. Used not on floors but as hangings and space dividers inside tents, they were, like the Unicorn tapestries, easy to transport. They were also easy to manufacture, and every tribal family would have its own sheep for wool, as well as its own spindles and looms. As with tartans, patterns and colors handed down through the generations from mother to daughter became identified with individual tribes, and they were never made for sale (nor were they collected in the West much before the twentieth century).

Peculiar to Anatolia, central and southwestern Turkey, is the "slit-weave" method of weaving, so called because of the gap left along the warp between blocks of color where the weft yarn has to turn back on itself. Various solutions were used to keep this slit as short as possible, from using serrated edges to incorporating as many diagonal lines in the design as possible. The tribal weavers practically never turned to curvilinear styles of arabesques (though they were used for the Ottoman court) which reduce the problem, preferring to stick to the abstract geometric patterns whose hard edges exaggerated the contrasts of color zones.

The weavers' highly evolved sense of color balance, developed long before abstract fine art came along, was aided by the soft tones and the uneven colorations, known appreciatively as *abrash*, achieved with natural dyes. As in medieval European tapestries, these included only three basic groups: madder (reds, purples, and browns), indigo (blues and greens), and weld (yellows). Indigo was the only dye not locally available in Turkey and was probably brought by itinerant professional dyers. This is why it is used only in relatively small quantities. (Woad did grow there but only has one thirtieth of the actual coloring agent, indicum.)

Red is by far the most dominant color. Whether this is due to the wide availability of madder or to convention is not known (though red was the favorite color of both Byzantine and Ottoman Turkey). It was an old tradition that disputes be settled "on a red carpet," suggesting ritualistic associations, and symbols such as the abstracted figure with "hands-on-hips" and the *mihrab* (niche) have been interpreted as the pagan fertility goddess and the cave where she lived respectively. It is assumed that the colors, too, of kilims are like a secret language that has survived enforced conversion to Christianity and Islam but has yet to be decoded.

Though kilims are still woven, often on traditional looms, the shadowy intensity of the colors and the rich textural effects of abrash, which gives such apparent depth to the tones, has been largely lost with the introduction of synthetic dyes between 1875 and 1914. The more even dyeing capabilities and brighter colors of these dyes exaggerate even minor color disharmonies; and since dyeing instructions were often poorly grasped by non-literate tribeswomen, resulting color instability has also destroyed carefully calculated color balances. A movement within Turkey, as in the West, is trying to gather the last remnants of knowledge and to reestablish traditional (and, unfortunately, very labor-intensive) dyeing techniques.

Anatolian kilim, late nineteenth century. Still using the basic red dye of the madder plant and a range of natural dye colors that, before the arrival of synthetics, had remained essentially unchanged for several millennia. The palette is close to that of Coptic textiles, but white (or beige) is relatively unimportant to the design. Kilim courtesy ABC Carpet and Home, New York.

31 | China's Hand-Painted Wallpapers

From Han dynasty (220 BC–AD 202) silks to Ming (1368–1644) porcelain, the appeal of Chinese products and their colors in the West has been remarkable. Sèvres was certainly influenced by the showy enamel colors of Kangxi (Qing dynasty emperor, 1662–1722) polychrome porcelain, particularly the *familles rose* and *vert*; and serene Song dynasty (960–1279) celadon may have precipitated the soft gray-greens of eighteenth century European—and thus also American—interiors. One of China's most influential and, today, little known exports were the wallpapers that may have appeared in Europe as early as the seventeenth century but were highly prized both there and in America in the eighteenth and nineteenth centuries, spurring home-grown industries for paper wall covering.

Chinese wallpapers were made of joined sheets of mulberry paper yielding panels mostly a standard forty-seven inches wide and ten to twelve feet high and usually sold in sets of twenty to twenty-five. Mounted on silk, heavy cartridge paper, or linen, they were shipped in rolls to the West. Outlined by hand in simple carbon ink and then filled in with colored washes, the images never used repeat patterns, making every set essentially unique and expensive. The most common type of papers included highly stylized, anti-perspective scenes of blossoming trees or bamboo, often growing from fantastic rock formations, with animals, birds, and insects depicted in great detail and all in bright, naturalistic colors. Extra sheets of birds or butterflies would often be sold with each set; these sheets could be cut and pasted over torn or stained sections.

In general, the Chinese designs were painted on ungrounded papers so that there were less surface paints that could flake off when rolled and transported. The resulting soft white or creamy colored grounds that characterize the oldest papers were a large factor in the airiness that these papers would lend to a room. Sometimes, however, the paper would be tinted in the pulp stage, creating soft blues and pinks equally effective at setting off the strong black calligraphic lines and subtly changing the mood from warm to cool. This tinting method was replaced by a vogue for laid-in grounds in the early eighteenth century.

Everyone who was anyone wanted at least one room decorated with the "India" papers (as they were often known, since Britain's East India Company was the largest importer), even going as far as building rooms to fit the standard panels exactly. Even George Washington, always fashion conscious, is on record as having ordered a set for Mount Vernon in 1787.

Hand-painted scenic wallpaper panels, eighteenth-century Chinese. Many American interiors were graced with these fine decorative papers. Designs could be custom ordered, but the colors almost always came from a characteristically Chinese palette. Courtesy Cooper Hewitt National Museum of Design, Smithsonian Institution—Art Resource, NY. Gift of Mrs. Harry Paine Bingham.

The papers inspired a host of imitators, who brought in woodblock printing technology to bring prices down.

Even more whimsical and fantastic than true Chinese ornament, chinoiserie certainly influenced rococo and there are whole interiors, including furniture, decorated in the "Chinese taste" at Capodimonte, Italy, and Aranjuez, Spain, and most famously at the Royal Pavilion, Brighton, England. Largely designed by John Nash, architect for the Prince Regent (later King George IV), this farmhouse-turned-Eastern-pleasure-palace is a curious hybrid of Gothic (with which Nash was more familiar) and Indian, as well as Chinese architecture, featuring remarkable interiors full of cast-iron staircases painted to look like bamboo, original Chinese painted wallpapers, and large quantities of lacquered furniture. Much of this was executed in the fairly authentic palette, shown here, of apple green, yellow, rose red, and ultramarine blue, as well as the coral, paler green, and lavender that had become popular in China in the late-eighteenth century, and a very pale version of the turquoise blue. All the colors are light and airy, a strong contrast to the heavy and dull colors that had begun to dominate in the Regency period.

By the time the Pavilion was finished in 1823, popular interest in chinoiserie had waned following the neoclassical reaction to rococo ornament (see Adam Brothers' Classicism, page 40). It had a brief resurgence in the 1860s when Anglo-French victories over China in the Second Opium War (1857–1860) resulted in a flood of artifacts into Europe, and when Owen Jones retracted his unfavorable opinion of Chinese art in his 1867 book, *Examples of Chinese Ornament Selected from Objects in the South Kensington Museum and Other Collections*. However, chinoiserie was soon to be superseded forever by a new interest in japaneserie (see Japan's Ukiyo-e woodblocks, page 66).

32 | **Paisley's Indian Roots**

Paisley, a town in southern Scotland, was a center of the nineteenth-century cotton industry. It gave its name to a fabric design that in fact evolved in northern India. The distinctive paisley teardrop motif is based on the *boteh* (from the Hindi *buta*, flower), itself a stylized plant form found woven in seventeenth and eighteenth century Kashmiri shawls. Imported by the East India Company in the early 1800s, these were soon a fashion necessity among the very wealthy English. In fact, a fine shawl, as much as five years in the making, could cost as much as a London townhouse.

In Indian originals the boteh was used sparingly, usually against a plain cream or red background, most often as a motif around the borders. To bring the fabric more into line with the prevailing taste for allover design, Western designers were hired to develop patterns, first for Indian weavers and then for the burgeoning industry in Paisley, that could make shawls at a fraction of the price. The result, a curious blend of East and West, was the familiar style in which the forms flow around one another in characteristic profusion, and a palette of colors which refers both to Victorian England and to India. It was a huge success. With slight changes of size, shape, density, and colors to accommodate fashion's vicissitudes, "paisleys" kept their overall distinctive look and popularity into the twentieth century.

Possibly because both Kashmir and England have a temperate to cold climate, the paisley palette tended to hold true to richly bold and deep saturated hues, not unlike those found in tartans. Almost all paisleys key off a deep red, rust, or maroon, and modern paisleys tend to be interpreted—often in prints rather than wovens—in graded reddish tones, often ending in browns. The initial Scottish dyers, however, used a wide range of colors for dyeing, and later printing, paisleys of wool, cotton, jute and linen. These included pink, pale indigo blue, orange-yellow, and an Indian muted emerald green, although Victorian combinations often had black as a ground to deepen the overall effect.

Paisley shawl, showing the red or rust, yellow and black that occur most frequently in this Indian-derived pattern.

...Only for the moment, gazing at the moon, snow, cherry blossoms and autumn wine, women and song, floating along with the current of life, like a gourd floating down a river.
— Sai Ryoi, from *Ukiyo Monogatari* (Tales of the Floating World)

33 | Japan's Ukiyo-e Woodblocks

Ukiyo-e, "pictures of the floating world," are the Japanese woodblock prints of the seventeenth through the nineteenth centuries. These prints, made during the stable prosperity of the Tokugawa Shogunate, have had a profound influence on the Impressionists and Post-Impressionists (see Monet, Seurat, Whistler), as well as art lovers and graphic designers.

Outstanding ukiyo-e artists include Hishikawa Moronobu (1618–1694), who popularized the single sheet print in black and white (*chimai-e*) among the growing merchant class of Edo (now Tokyo); Suzuki Harunobu (1725–1770), whose work is associated with the first *nishiki*, or brocade-like polychromatic prints; Ando Hiroshige (1797–1858), known for his travelogue prints; Kitagawa Utamaro (1753–1806), specialist in *bijin-ga*, portraits of female beauty; Katsushika Hokusai (1760–1849), well known for dramatic blue and white seascapes; and Utagawa Kuniyoshi (1798–1861), the nineteenth-century colorist of action prints featuring animals and birds.

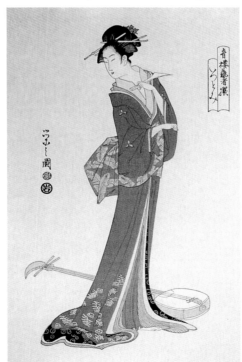

Whimsical, at times erotic, and always, even at their most full-blown, quite refined, ukiyo-e initially used just one color (generally *tan*, a vermilion rose from red lead), and then two (red and green, the red, *beni*, closer to crimson and derived from saffron), before adding purple and yellow. Hand-colored until the introduction of printing in color c. 1740, ukiyo-e prints in their full polychromatic form used up to thirty blocks by 1765. Additional color effects were achieved through painting over a glaze incorporating mica crystals which gave a frosty iridescence;

Kunisada, *A Lady of the Edo Court*. Original nineteenth century print showing the characteristically soft tones associated with ukiyo-e woodblocks. Courtesy Old Japan, Inc., New York.

through gauffrage, an embossing technique using un-inked woodblocks to give relief or spatial effects to white snow; and through gofan, a white pigment made from chalk of powdered shells that was mixed with paints and rendered tints more neutral. The palette is a beautiful example of Japanese taste for *shibui*—muted, soft—color effects. The soft tones, notably rose reds, subdued greens, buffs, whites, plum browns, mellow indigos, and grays, executed in water-color pigments, are delightfully enriched by the textured surfaces of handmade papers often made

Ando Hiroshige, *Maple Trees with Tekona Shrine and Bridges*, c.1850s. One of the one hundred famous views of Edo (Tokyo); Hiroshige died during the production of this series, the culmination of his career, and the group was finished by his pupils. Reprint from original woodblocks. The bright colors may be close to what the inks looked like before fading. Courtesy Old Japan, Inc., New York.

from mulberry bark. Nevertheless, many old ukiyo-e prints may have been considerably brighter at the time they were executed than they are today; blues and purples particularly, being fugitive colors, have tended to fade to off-grays and muddy browns. The surprising pinks and electric blues of this modern reprint of a Hiroshige landscape are considered reasonably authentic. If the softer colors caught Whistler's eye (see page 134), these brights would have impressed the Impressionists.

Victorian Decoratives

The great age of polychromy, the art of using many colors. Inspired by sources ranging from medieval cathedrals to Islamic palaces, by revelations of colorful Greek temples and Pompeiian murals, and working with a large number of new pigments, the ever-romantic Victorians developed color into an extraordinary tool of personal and cultural expression.

34 | Shaker Minimalism

The Shaker palette—and their minimalist design aesthetic—is sometimes considered a reaction to the brash styles of the Victorian era. However, while the appeal of Shaker design reached its height in the mid-nineteenth century, the origins of this religious sect dates back to the 1770s; thus the palette is closely related to that of colonial America.

Founded by "Mother" Ann Lee, a English immigrant, the first small community was established near Albany, New York. Known originally, and derisively, as the "Shaking Quakers" for the way they would tremble with religious ecstasy, the Shakers established a model communal society which promoted simplicity, even austerity.

Handicrafts were an integral part of the Shaker life and all members were expected to develop several skills with their hands. The driving principle of Shaker design was purity of form and absence of superfluous decoration. However, the simplicity of design belied the extreme care that went into the manufacture of anything from tables to fabrics, as well as an eye for subtle and graceful detail. Every last element of Shaker interiors, from peg racks on the walls to unprecedented numbers of built-in drawers and cupboards for storage, was fully thought out to further the sublime harmony that characterizes their interiors.

The importance of the palette lies as much in how it was used as in individual colors. The Shakers distinguished themselves by using paint sparingly, particularly for furniture which was generally oiled to bring out the natural tones of the woods or painted in a single color. Interiors and exteriors were painted all white or cream, and a single sober color was chosen as an accent, to be used only on shutters and trim. The result was a Japanese-like harmony of natural woods, white, and earth colors or black, as in the omnipresent cast-iron stoves.

Architecturally, red and yellow were the least used colors, except that red was a characteristic color for barns, helping to capture the sun's warmth in winter. Red was also a common, and usefully dirt-hiding, color for clothes, and both red and yellow were used for textiles such as the web strap seats for chairs and as stains applied directly to wooden storage boxes as a welcome, if only occasional, warm color accent.

Traditional oval nesting boxes still made by the Shaker Workshops of Concord, Massachusetts, showing the characteristic soft, grayed primaries that are rustic but authentic American colors first used during the colonial era.

*There is one color . . . frequently employed by house painters, which we feel bound to
protest* against *most heartily, as entirely unsuitable, and in bad taste. This is WHITE..."*
—Andrew Jackson Downing, architect, 1842

35 | Victorian Painted Ladies

It would have been surprising if Victorian architects, after richly decorating
their houses with exotic detailing, *had* left them white, although white had
been the most popular color—with green for shutters—for Greek Revival
houses around the 1820s.

The difference was a revolutionary new building method called wood
balloon-framing, invented in Chicago in the 1830s and still used today,
which provided affordable housing for the emerging middle class of the
Industrial Revolution. While most houses were built from mail-order
catalogues and pattern books, the system was enormously flexible and each
house could be personalized to suit the buyer's taste. Exuberant color matched
the quirky fretwork and filigree, decorative shingle patterns, turrets, bay
windows and porches that turned houses into early Disneylands of personal
imagination. Art was a means of self-improvement, and choosing and decorating a home was a means by which an individual was supposed to raise
himself above the banality of his factory or office job.

The expressive use of color was fully a part of this process. At first, in the
Gothic Revival style popularized by Downing, colors were restrained. The
body of the house was painted in a palette that was medieval in origin; it
included stone and brick colors ranging from light earthy colors and honey
browns to tans and slate grays, with trim in the same hue but a darker shade
and shutters still in green. By the mid-1850s, according to the Italianate and
Stick styles, deeper colors were being introduced, including yellows, blue-
grays, terra-cotta reds, maroons, and ochers. Trim started to appear in
contrasting colors of evergreens, browns, yellows, and creams, and shutters
were now sometimes brown. In general, window sashes were painted in
dark colors to make the window seem to drop behind the ornamented facade.

The height of Victorian decoration came from the 1870s onward, when
quantities of cheap new synthetic pigments were coming on the market
and ready-mixed pigments were available
(previously they had been laboriously
mixed by hand). Queen Anne-style houses
were appearing in harmonies of three to
five colors, which now included buttercup
yellow, bottle blue-green, crimson, and
dark blues. Colors were all used to emphasize asymmetrical lines and varied textures,
with the brighter tones usually reserved
for trim and window sashes.

**Second Empire-style house with mansard,
c. 1886. Three colors, straw, medium
brownstone, and fawn, are used to contrast
body and architectural detailing; they
coordinate harmoniously with the deep
red of the shingles. Window trim is characteristically dark to accentuate apparent
depth of the openings. Collection of Mr.
and Mrs. Lewis Seely, The Anthenaeum
of Philadelphia.**

It can be difficult to reproduce the deep, deep tones of Victorian house paints, particularly the resonant shutter greens, because the natural linseed, nut, and poppy oils, which could take two weeks or more to set, are no longer used as binders, replaced by faster drying mineral oils and acrylic. Nor are many such deep tones available from paint manufacturers. Experts recommend mixing your own colors in the old tradition, starting with a not-too-dark factory base and then gradually mixing in lighter, standard, factory-ground colors.

| **Owen Jones—Ornament's Grammarian**

In the mid-nineteenth century, color was not the frivolous, distracting entity that many would see it as later; rather it was of central importance and, as suggested by Chevreul, Runge, and Goethe's studies, subject to quasi-scientific enquiry.

Owen Jones (1809–1874), a British architect and decorator, was the most important theoretician on architectural design and its coloration in the nineteenth century. He made a pioneering study of the Moorish palace of the Alhambra in 1836 (see Moorish Spain's Tiles, page 52), one of the first design books to make use of chromolithography for color reproduction. His subsequent book, *The Grammar of Ornament* (1856), was the first systematic survey of ornamental pattern and color around the world. Emphasizing the importance of balanced, two-dimensional design with no attempt at shadow or relief, its plates—and perhaps their idiosyncratic, none too true colorations, too—were a huge influence on the Arts and Crafts Movement, whose members were struggling to reform the muddled, vulgarian quality of mass-produced design.

In the tradition of the time, Jones proposed very precise rules governing the architectural use of color, including

1. Ornament for flat surfaces should be stylized with no distracting highlights and shadows "tempting you to pluck it from the surface."

2. Primary colors are all important; a preference for a palette of secondary or tertiary colors indicates a decadent civilization.

3. Color should be used to define form, "to distinguish objects or parts of objects one from another," as it was on Egyptian temples, Moorish mosques or Gothic cathedrals.

4. Colors should be isolated from each other (as in tilework or stained glass windows); contrasting colors should be edged in light tones; combinations with gold or yellow should be edged in black.

5. Color schemes must be properly balanced so that "every colour or tint, from the palest and most delicate to the deepest and richest shades, [receives] just the amount of ornaments that it is adapted to bear."

In the last case, Jones proposed that primary colored areas should be used in the proportions of eight parts blue, five red, and three yellow, so that stronger colors are toned down by deeper blue. Similarly, for secondaries, eight parts orange, thirteen purple, and eleven green; and for tertiaries, nineteen parts citrine (orange/green mix), twenty-one russet, and twenty-four olive. If used in the correct balance, he assured the reader, they would blend optically at a distance "[to] present a neutralized bloom." Almost offhandedly, Jones added that each color was rarely found fully saturated, and that lighter or grayer colors needed proportionately larger areas to have the same effect; he could give no mathematical guidelines to today's colorist who, even in a simple color atlas, has several hundred minute variations of shades and tints to use.

Despite the limitations of printing technology, the small color range illustrated in *The Grammar of Ornament* does show some of the combinations that were exceedingly popular in Victorian England, particular the creamy yellow, quarry-tile red, brown, and black (and sometimes green) derived from medieval floor tiles and used for encaustic tiles by Minton since 1835. The stronger colors had also been put to work by Jones himself, whose controversial paint scheme for the cast-iron columns and struts of the Crystal Palace, built for the 1851 Great Exhibition, included "harmonious" proportions of yellow, red, and blue, often in stripes, which up close helped define the individual elements of the structure but which blended at normal viewing distances into a vibrant blue-gray haze.

Stuccoed, four-story house, Great Russell Street, London. Repainted in the original Victorian Palette developed by Owen Jones, the building shows how strong color contrasts were used in the polychromatic style to define architectural elements and ornamental details. These colors were used largely for cast-iron structures such as railroad stations.

37

William Morris's Refined Decoratives

A harsh critic of Victorian excess, English poet and artist William Morris spent much of his career fulminating against the clutter and the useless status symbols of the emerging industrial middle classes—the cheap mass-produced reproductions and the new garish synthetic dyes and pigments. Amidst the endless revivals, from neoclassicism to neo-gothicism, he focused on one period known for its simplicity and, to him, its honesty of design: the Middle Ages.

An admirer of medieval tapestries, Morris painstakingly researched and recreated the colors used. He rejected the emerging synthetic dyes as being too harsh, and he extensively researched natural dyes, making the palette of greens of every cast the centerpiece of his own range, together with deep indigo blue and strong madder red. These colors were featured throughout his handwoven fabrics and his famous wallpapers, which he saw as affordable replacements for tapestries and frescoes respectively.

The patterns are all complex, rich and naturalistic—at first glance not all that different from the ornate furnishing being used in many interiors of Victorian England (see Victorian Overstuffed Interiors, page 50). However, Morris's interior design sense was based on the medieval original: stripped down rooms accented with a single colorful wallhanging or wallpainting. He shocked many of his associates by painting interiors all white, including the ubiquitous Victorian paneling, using the natural tones of exposed brick and wood trim, together with restrained application of his papers and upholstery fabrics as color accents. This was to be highly influential on the Modern Movement and did in fact contribute to the lightening of interiors in the 1880s.

In keeping with his move away from the gloomy Victorian interiors—darkness was a sign of wealth; it meant investing in a lot of candles, and it also kept the skin a "civilized" white—Morris's colors are, by the standards of the time, light and breezy. This quality was heightened by the use of strong color contrasts and of cream or white for wall surfaces that were painted, instead of wallpapered. The pink, yellow, and pale blue of the papers are particularly light and fresh; these pretty colors were used for more "feminine" applications, such as for drawing rooms and bedrooms, while the deeper tones were intended for the more "masculine" libraries and dining rooms. Morris's most characteristic patterns in printed cotton are the gray-blue, yellow-green, cream, and bright red accent of "Strawberry Thief" (1883) and the soft tonal greens with subtle pink in "Daffodil" (1891).

Modern reproduction of William Morris's **Willow Boughs, c. 1860s.** These grayed colors, along with Morris's medieval deeps, used in allover patterns on fabrics and on wallpapers, were typical of the Morris & Co. workshop's output, highly influential on the Arts and Crafts movement. Courtesy Arthur Sanderson & Sons, London/New York.

The story of tartans is part history, part myth. The oldest illustrated record of their distinctive designs and clan affiliations, the manuscript *Vestiarium Scoticum* (Scottish Dress), "discovered" in 1842, was widely discredited as a forgery even at the time of its publication. This did not dampen the enthusiasm of Victorians, however, for a genuinely "British" fabric, and so Scottish and English mills were soon churning out huge quantities of these plaid fabrics. Queen Victoria herself sealed tartan's popularity by covering the walls and furniture of her summer home in Scotland with the "Balmoral Tartan," designed by her consort, Prince Albert, shortly after the estate was bought in 1852.

Woolen plaid *breacans* (Gaelic for checkered or variegated fabrics; *tartaine*, from which tartan is derived, is French) do in fact date back to the Middle Ages, and they use the basic palette of strong greens, reds, and yellows set against muted blues and grays. However, the distinctive *sett*, or arrangement of intersecting stripes, tended to identify a weaving center, and secondarily, a clan, because the colors depended on local availability of dyes and on regional traditions. For instance, fabrics from western Scotland (such as the MacLeod or Campbell) are often blue-green based while their northern cousins (such as the Mackintosh or Grant) typically have a red ground.

As in Persian carpets, the natural dye colors could be extremely bright, but they are often found, and preferred, in their faded state. The sources are orchil, madder, and lichen for reds and purples (reds overdyed with blues); tree barks and lichen for browns; woad for blue; alder roots for black; and nettles or overdyes of blue and yellow for green. Victorians liked their colors soberly dark, to the point that tartan blues and greens were almost black. A reaction to these blackened Victorian tartans resulted in a revival of the softer tones of so-called "ancient color," using, in fact, synthetic dyes, after the First World War. In England and America, the livelier versions (as shown here) with cleaner colors have generally been preferred.

The pre-determined grid of intersecting stripes provides an unusual exercise in the purely abstract use of color. The contrasting blocks of color, the changing tones where stripes intersect, are reminiscent of Albers's experiments with color interaction at the Bauhaus (see Josef Albers, page 90). The geometric forms and dramatic palette of muted primaries, the expressive tools of an artisan's sensibility, perfectly counterpoint the original, coarse-textured plain weaves for which they were designed.

Buchanan tartan.

MacIntyre tartan.

39 | **Liberty & Co. Prints**

From a modest beginning in 1875 at 218A Regent Street, London, Liberty & Co. developed into a major design influence in late-Victorian London and Paris, creating a demand for so-called "Art Colours," the delicate off-tints of Far Eastern art and printed silks.

The founder of Liberty & Co., Arthur Lasenby Liberty, who originally named his shop The East India House, effectively changed middle-class fashion and interior decoration by offering oriental exotica at affordable prices. He began by importing silks, later adding curios, carpets, lamps, and some furniture. Chinese and Japanese silks were especially popular, and demand soon far outpaced supply. Since materials from Asia were also fragile and dyes often fugitive, and because Eastern producers were themselves being influenced by aniline-dyed European cloths and starting to use bolder color schemes, Liberty turned to manufacturing sources at home.

Many of Liberty's early fabrics were commissioned from Arthur Silver, founder of the first English design studio. Like William Morris and the later Aesthetic Movement, which argued for "rational dress" with a non-constricting design and colored by soft, natural dyes, he reacted against the violent purples, greens, and reds that characterized the first synthetic dyes. While Silver favored the softer, complex tones of vegetable dyes, he was responsive to the contemporary taste for brighter color, and his combinations are alive and sometimes almost iridescent, though generally based on just three colors (with white) chosen from a range of deep blues, ocher oranges, strong reds, and soft to medium greens.

The remarkable tonal harmonies of the designs were a great commercial success, sported by Wilde and Whistler and even appearing in the original 1881 production of Gilbert and Sullivan's *Patience*, to great acclaim. The fabrics were of such high quality that "Liberty" almost became synonymous with a finely printed material.

From the 1920s, Liberty fabrics, such as the Tana Lawn or "little floral" series, moved from slightly dusky to clearer colors. The palette was increasingly based on more feminine light to middle tones—pink corals, peaches, lavenders, slate blues, and grassy greens, played off poppy red and an occasional sophisticated taupe, muted yellow, or dark navy blue. Delicate and pretty in the best sense of the word, Liberty's florals also became instant classics; by the thirties they were being ordered as dress material for

Princesses Elizabeth and Margaret; in the sixties and seventies, the French, notably Cacherel and Daniel Hechter, used Liberty's printed florals extensively. These fabrics continue to be prized for their gentle hues, soft outlines, and the quality of their color application.

Liberty print fabric, cotton, reproduction of a 1900 design. The peacock feather motif was developed by Liberty's principal designer, Arthur Silver, although this particular colorway was by his son, Rex Silver; the peacock feather was also the signature motif of the Aesthetic Movement. The Silvers' designs, well suited to the material, were intended to be practical in form and color.

| **Tiffany's Modern Stained Glass**

Louis Comfort Tiffany's (1848–1933) exquisite blown glass hues, ranging from opaque greens and golds to opalescents and pale, milky pastels, are a rich lode of Art Nouveau colors used between 1892 and 1928. His colors and forms reflect an obsession with representing nature and incorporating scaled, low-contrast harmonies and undulating line.

Tiffany studied under George Innes, the American landscape painter. He was also influenced by William Morris and Owen Jones, and when he established a decorating firm in 1879, he created interiors with curious blends of Byzantine, Moorish, and Romanesque styles. Patenting in 1880 a type of hand-blown iridescent glass which he called "favrile," he went on to establish the Tiffany Furnaces, for which he became famous, in Corona (Queens), New York in 1892.

The output of the factory can be divided roughly into three periods: 1892–1900 was a period of experimentation, in which the velvety effect of iridescent glass and rich opaque golds, saturated blues, and deep greens were explored; 1900–1918 saw the brightest colors (shown here) produced in glass and enamels for windows, lamps, vases, pottery, and candlesticks; 1918–1928 was "the Nash Period," featuring the pastel colors favored by Arthur J. Nash, the plant manager.

Though under the direct control of Tiffany himself, the plant involved many other hands in developing the colors, including the Venetian Andrea Boldini, under whom Tiffany had trained at the Heidt glasshouse in Brooklyn; Arthur E. Saunders, whose specialty was aquamarine glass; the chemist Dr. Parker McIlhenny, who remained at Tiffany's for twenty years; and George J. Cook, who developed the formula for peacock glass.

The Tiffany palette is dominated by peony red, dragonfly white, grape purple, peacock and wisteria blues, tulip yellow, olive green, and rose pink. Dramatized by metallized iridescence, color laid upon color, and chance color effects from the fumes and chemicals, the pieces have a striking lushness of tone. Like leafy arbors, the leaded-glass shades—developed to soften the harsh new electric lights—provide the best lessons in how the colors were combined, whether as simple progressions of yellow and blue or in the complex tonal poems in blue, green, yellow, and purple that evoke Monet's *Water Lilies* (see Monet, page 136).

Louis Comfort Tiffany, lamp with Cabbage Rose leaded-glass shade and bronze base, c.1900–1915. Produced in the Tiffany Studios in Corona, Long Island, the naturalistic motifs of the lamp are set off by the complementary harmony of pale rose pinks against a background of deep forest greens. Courtesy The Corning Museum of Glass, gift of Mrs. Madelein Falk.

Shades of the Machine Age

From Cubist drabs to Deco brilliants, a new culture dominated by the automobile and airplane, by themes of speed and mechanization, develops a love-hate relationship with color, finding beauty and truth both in shades of dingy neutrals and in hard-edged industrial brights.

41 | **Frank Lloyd Wright**

The architecture and interiors of Frank Lloyd Wright (1867–1959) are the natural extension of nineteenth century Arts and Crafts ideals, as he believed in unity of design, honesty to materials, and the democratic possibilities of architecture if good design were made available to everyone. Where he broke with the tradition was to express a commitment to new, machine processes, the old bugbear of theorists like Ruskin and Morris. "The machine," he declared at a meeting of the Chicago Society of Arts and Crafts in 1901, "by its wonderful cutting, shaping, smoothing, and repetitive capacity, has made it possible to so use it without waste that the poor as well as the rich may enjoy today beautiful surface treatments of clean, strong forms."

Paint and wallpaper, considered somehow aesthetically dishonest, and with them the strong colors of the Victorian era, were largely banished. The natural tones of wood—his favorites were the orangy tones of cypress for trim, red or white oak for furniture, and long-leaf yellow pine for floors— took on particular significance, along with unadorned brick or concrete (though the floors of his Usonian houses of the 1930s and 1940s were stained red to match brickwork) as the unifying factor of his interiors.

While the Usonians tended to work off red and orange, Wright's earliest Prairie style was characterized by yellow and green, and color was used relatively liberally. Coordinated schemes were carefully

Frank Lloyd Wright, Taliesin West, Living Room looking toward south, 1938. Several of the striped pillows were made by famed American textile designer Dorothy Liebes especially for Frank Lloyd Wright.

developed in each house with colors of the walls echoed in carpets and stained-glass windows. Paints were applied in thin stains to the stucco

Frank Lloyd Wright, Taliesin West, living room looking east.

or mixed in with the plaster itself. Wright's favored choices appear to have been a goldenrod yellow, a medium green not unlike colonial verdigris green, a pale olive green, and a "Cherokee red," later to feature in the signature red square logo on his architectural drawings. Exterior stucco was also often stained soft olive or yellow, emphasizing the way his low-slung houses appeared to grow organically out of the landscape.

Where stronger color did consistently pop up—in stained glass windows of the earlier houses and in carpets—Wright continued the analogy with nature in soft, foliage-like reds and greens, and watery blues set off against large neutral or creamy white grounds. Wright's affinity for simple or restrained colors and for geometry, particularly the most basic forms such as diamonds, squares, and circles that are recurrent themes in windows and furnishings alike, is heavily influenced by the stylized arts of Japan and by the rhythmic structures of nature that he strove to capture throughout his career.

42 | SoHo Cast-Iron Deeps

The use of cast iron for columns dates back to the 1790s in England when they were first used in textile mills because of their fire resistance. By the early 1800s, cast iron's great strength and ability to be cast in molds led John Nash to incorporate tall and extremely thin cast-iron columns in the kitchens of the Royal Pavilion, topped with wrought iron foliage that gave them the appearance of palm trees.

Cast-iron architecture took off in New York after James Bogardus demonstrated in 1849 a way to construct a complete building out of individually cast architectural parts, including columns, lintels, and panels, at the corner of New York's Duane and Center Streets. The frame construction also meant that windows could be disproportionately large, allowing more light into the deep interiors. Cast iron proved a remarkably cheap method of building, and the mass production of identical interchangeable elements that could be assembled on site was the origin of modern architecture and today's skyscrapers.

Cast in molds, the iron easily took decorative motifs and the stylish ornamentation that gave simple factory buildings an aura of grandeur. This was a great part of cast iron's appeal in the Victorian age. Cornices, pediments, keystones, and balustrades based on carved stone originals were manufactured at a fraction of the price, and gave much the same effect as stone. In fact, where other materials weathered and deteriorated, iron was remarkably strong and resistant and could be freshened with a single coat of paint.

Protective Polychromy

Paint was, from the start, an integral part of cast-iron architecture, because iron is vulnerable in one particular area—without a protective coat it will quickly rust. A coat of primer paint was applied straight after casting at the foundry in preparation for shipping. After assembly, the whole building was then painted in a dark, opaque coat of oil paint to hide scuffs and to further protect the vulnerable surface. Incorporating the prevailing ideas on polychromy, the original buildings were painted in fashionable dusky tones with architectural details picked out in naturalistic colors (see Victorian Painted Ladies, page 70).

Today, New York, and in particular the SoHo district, represents the largest collection of intact cast-iron buildings in the world, thanks to a preservation effort launched in the 1960s. Some of the buildings have been repainted in original colors, but many of the paint schemes now reflect the colors of cheap enamel paints of the early to mid-twentieth century, though white, which is now affordable for the first time, is increasingly popular. Unfortunately, the details are almost never highlighted with color due to the cost of labor—a factor that previously contributed to cast iron's disappear-

ance in favor of rolled steel. The palette shown here represents a survey of colors used today, which range from deep grayed blues and greens to dark red or maroon, "drab," a brown made by adding burnt umber, Indian red, and a little black to white, according to Andrew Jackson Downing, and an occasional brighter (but still grayed) green.

Characteristic grayed but deep colors used on the cast-iron "loft" buildings of New York. These are, in fact, the colors of industrial paints of the mid–twentieth century. Increasingly the facades are being "cleaned up" with a coat of white paint, which was not an original nineteenth-century color.

. . . neither Picasso nor Braque was interested, as Monet supremely was, in the effects of light . . . [but in] matter—that plasma, the colour of guitar backs, zinc bars, and smokers' fingers, of which the Cubist world was composed.
—Robert Hughes, in *Shock of the New*, 1980

43 | Cubism: The Industrial Palette

Like Leonardo's work, the Cubist movement was an anti-color revolution, concerned with exploring three-dimensional form and space on canvas without the symbolic language and aesthetic beauty that color can bring to a painting.

In a most unusual artistic collaboration, Pablo Picasso and Georges Braque worked closely together for six years, largely in Paris, from 1908 until Braque was called up by the French army in August 1914, stimulating and often appropriating each other's ideas. Although Braque had been a Fauve and a disciple of Cézanne, together they developed a palette which dominates their most austere period of 1908–1912 (now labeled "analytic cubism") of gray, black, and white. Yet even at its darkest and most intense, cubism never completely closed the door on color: somber gray-greens counterbalanced by warm tones of cream and brown kept on creeping in to add to the textural richness of the paintings.

Workman Aesthetic

In fact, from 1910 on, Picasso, Spanish and naturally vivacious, began to make serious efforts to reintroduce color, but always ended up painting it out. It was the taciturn Frenchman, Braque, who made the innovation that opened the way to color: this was *collage*. As they moved into "synthetic" Cubism over the course of 1912, both artists started sticking new materials onto their paintings, from brown wrapping paper to newsprint, wallpaper, sand, and earth. Less concerned with spatial depth, they began to find a role for color to define surface planes; of course, these colors tended to be muted. Still rejecting the fine pigments favored by the Impressionists and Fauves, and often affecting the role of working-class heroes in blue overalls, they used simple housepainters' enamel colors popular at the time, including a deep green, a rose, and a gray-blue.

After the war, in which Braque suffered a severe head wound, the two moved apart. While Picasso returned to developing his natural abilities as a draftsman, Braque stuck with formal Cubism, working alongside a new generation of Cubists, including Metzinger and Gris. While neither Picasso nor Braque would take the final step toward abstraction— their paintings always *represented* something, be it a landscape, still-life, or person—Cubism was particularly influential on the development of abstract art.

Pablo Picasso, *Daniel-Henry Kahnweiler*, 1910. Oil on Canvas. Dingy browns and cool grays, the colors of smoke-filled bars and modern factories, provided the means for the Cubist's exploration of matter and space. Courtesy The Art Institute of Chicago, Gift of Mrs. Gilbert W. Chapman, 1948.561

44 | The De Stijl Style

Characterized by a palette of primary red, yellow, and blue, the no-nonsense austerity of the Dutch de Stijl (The Style) movement, founded in 1917, was a response to the horrors and excesses of the First World War. Painters Piet Mondrian and Theo van Doesburg, the architect J.J.P. Oud, and designer Gerrit Rietveld believed in the spiritual power of abstraction and clear geometric forms to create a universal language of calm rationalism.

Unlike Cubism, color played an intrinsic role in their style, and the use of the primaries indicate the most important influence on the de Stijl artists: medieval stained glass (although the secondary colors also seen in that period are not used). Both Mondrian and Doesburg were well aware of the symbolic weight of red, yellow, and blue which appealed to strong emotions and had deep religious and cultural connotations (see Stained Glass Spirituals, page 12); they even used in their paintings heavy black outlining comparable to the leading of stained glass windows to heighten the intensity of the hues.

The principles of de Stijl were to apply to all the arts, and the de Stijl palette was used to particular effect in architecture, especially in the new open-plan interiors with simple, bare walls unadorned with any moldings. Flat areas of primary colors were used to emphasize the planar nature of the surfaces and to link together architectural elements from ceiling panels to doors and carpets. The colors were essentially used as accents against the broad expanses of white, so that the interiors were, as contemporary critics described them, colorful, but not excessively so. Also notable, though often now forgotten, are the tinted grays.

Piet Mondrian, *Composition with Red, Yellow and Blue*, 1930. Clashing, but minutely balanced primaries derived from medieval stained glass windows provide the palette that defines some Modernist aims in art and architecture, notably clarity and brevity. Giraudon/ Art Resource, New York.

In visual perception a color is almost never seen as it really is—as it physically is. This fact makes color the most relative medium in art. In order to use color effectively it is necessary to recognize that color deceives continually.
—Josef Albers, from Introduction to *Interaction of Color*, 1963

45 | Josef Albers: Interaction of Color

Teacher, theoretician, and artist, German-born Josef Albers (1888–1976) spent much of his life trying to pin down a good formal method for analyzing color's combinations as well as its more intangible expressive potential, an increasingly dominant concern of artists from Turner and Kandinsky to Matisse and America's Abstract Expressionists. His investigations became an important part of the "foundation" course Albers taught at the Bauhaus from 1923 to 1933.

Dissatisfied with dryly scientific theories of color harmony and perception, Albers recommended going back to basics and working with color chips to explore initially how colors can affect each other. In his seminal book *Interaction of Color* (1963), effectively a summation of his work at the Bauhaus and later at Black Mountain College in the United States, he notes that "practical exercises demonstrate through color deception (illusion) the relativity and instability of color." Because of the simultaneous contrast effect (in which a color's apparent brightness and even hue can be changed by a neighboring color), context becomes everything. Albers recommended working with paper, not only because it was cheap and easy, but also because the exact same color could be tried in a variety of situations and the colors were not affected by texture.

Using rectangles of colored paper, Albers explored contrast effects, illusions of space and transparency, and color temperature (the apparent warmth or coolness of colors). "Mixing" colors provided a particular challenge since this cannot be done the same way with paper as it can with paint; he made his students imagine the mixture of two colors and then find an actual example of that third color. Having done all this, one was then in a position to study the moods and ideas evoked by individual colors, color contrasts, and color progressions—happiness and sadness, youth and old age, discord and consonance, for example.

Josef Albers, *Homage to the Square; Carniferous*, 1958. Oil on composition. An interpretation in oil paints of Albers's work with colored paper at the Bauhaus and then at Yale. Courtesy The Museum of Modern Art, New York, Gift of Jay R. Braus.

Inevitably, perhaps, Albers was driven to translate his ideas back into paint, namely in his series *Homage to the Square*, begun in 1949. Each painting consisted of three to four nestled squares in which "color exists for color's sake" and the role of form is reduced to a minimum.

46 | **Art Deco Syncopation**

The color palette of Art Deco, a style named for the major 1925 Paris exhibition, *L'Exposition Internationale des Arts Décoratifs et Industriels*, was one of the last great flamboyant gestures of the twenties.

The sharp geometric motifs of Art Deco, also known as Jazz Modern or moderne, were charged with the syncopated rhythms of the new American music: color combinations counterpointed sophisticated neutrals of a distinctly technological or industrial origin—black, smoky white, and chrome (or gold)—with exaggerated brights culled from decorative sources as diverse as ancient Egyptian art (ocher, gold, and blue, a combination enormously popularized by the discovery of Tutankhamun's tomb in 1921), American Indian crafts (Navajo turquoise and Aztec jade green), and Russian costumes (the brilliant reds, oranges, and blues popularized by Bakst's Ballets Russes designs).

Where Art Nouveau had concentrated on handmade pieces produced for an elite audience, Art Deco was unabashedly consumer-oriented, manifesting itself in products ranging from furniture to tableware, in wood, steel, earthenware, and even plastic. While designs were increasingly pared down and rectilinear, color compensated by becoming more and more emboldened. Art Deco capitalized on the great Fauve achievement—the brilliant color effects that marked the break with naturalism and the move toward abstraction. This new dynamism swept away the seeming decadence of Nouveau's relatively delicate colors.

"Bizarre" Brights

Clarice Cliff (1899–1972), a leading designer of hand-painted ceramics for Wilkinson's, a Staffordshire, England, potter, exemplifies the broad range of shockingly bright hues in her early "Bizarre" line of the late 1920s, followed by the enormously popular "Crocus," "House and Bridge," and others of the 1930s. Her colors included a rich orange and a very similar red (often used interchangeably), greens varying from grayed to cucumber, a pinkish maroon, yellow, almost lilac blues, and a deep turquoise (largely in her "Inspiration" line, influenced by Persian ceramics). Cliff is relatively unusual in preferring allover color to the common Deco taste for a single bright with black against a white/cream ground. While all hues are vivid, they are more complex than

Clarice Cliff, Applique Avignon style, on an Eton teapot, a Lotus jug, and a punchbowl, 1930. Typical of her style, and of Art Deco in general, are clashing contrasts of exotic brights with oranges or orange-reds appearing prominently in many combinations. Courtesy Susan P. Meisel Decorative Arts, New York.

the brights we are used to today, largely because the Art Deco palette focuses on secondary and tertiary colors.

Because of the intensity of saturation, the palette enjoyed a popularity well beyond the 1930s among Americans, who have historically favored strong, bright colors. For example, 1940s fabrics, such as for curtains, often featured abstracted florals in signature deco coral reds, lime greens, and pearl grays. The palette was rediscovered in the sixties, ironically to be used largely in the packaging design of luxury items.

47 | **Pueblo Deco Theatricals**

Art Deco's influence in the early twentieth century was enormous. It was picked up by artists (see Diego Rivera, page 98) and architects across Europe and America, and sometimes even appeared reinterpreted in the very areas from which the colors had originally been drawn, including the Southwest of the United States, origin of the Navajo reds and turquoises so central to the Deco palette.

The Kimo (Isleta Pueblo for mountain lion or king of its kind) Theater in Albuquerque, New Mexico, presents an early (1927) example of Pueblo Deco. Exhibiting a wealth of decorative detailing, the Kimo draws its colors from various American sources including Pueblo architecture, Indian jewelry, and Hopi pottery, all combined in the Hollywood extravagance of a 1920s' theater palace.

Commissioned by an Italian immigrant and impresario called Oreste Bacheschi, the Kimo was designed by architect Carl Boller, who visited the Navajo and Hopi reservations, as well as several pueblos surrounding Albuquerque, for inspiration. Boller incorporated landscape murals in the interiors, as was done in many Art Deco

Kimo Theater, Albuquerque, New Mexico.
Art Deco mosaics showing Mayan influence.

skyscrapers, specially crafted silver kachina door handles, inlaid mosaic tiles, and architectural details painted in striking colors that helped define the structural parts of the building.

The Kimo depends heavily on the adobe tones of the region, largely a soft brown and a dark brown, replacing the traditional art deco black. Against this are highlighted the accent colors of deep turquoise blue, a traditional Pueblo as well as Navajo color, and orange, a mainstream Art Deco color.

Kimo Theater, Albuquerque, New Mexico. Kachina door handles in pewter.

Ornament has been, is and will be polychromatic; nature does not present us with any object that is monotonously uniform . . . therefore we must necessarily color, partially or completely, all architectonic members . . . Color in certain places has the great value of making the outlines and structural planes seem more energetic.
—Antonio Gaudi

48 | **Tropical Deco Resort**

The history of Miami Beach's Art Deco district has been and is again that of a tourist resort. Built largely during the 1930s on what had been a barrier island alongside a mangrove swamp until the end of the nineteenth century, South Beach, as it is now known, blossomed into a unique collection of deco hotels, apartments, and houses combining low-cost construction techniques with a populist style, specifically designed to draw middle-class tourists looking for an affordable holiday.

This "Depression Moderne" picked up its cues from the urban Deco movements up north, reinterpreting them for the subtropical south. Given its seaside location, the architecture followed the fashion for streamline design, particularly echoing the forms of contemporary steamships, incorporating recurring elements such as horizontal racing stripes molded into the stucco of the facades, cantilevered "eyebrow" sunshades over the windows, and stepped parapets.

Color was an important part of the exterior design, bringing a resort flair and sense of escape from the dreary depression-era times. The favorite colors were a sunny yellow, a sea green, and most distinctively a flamingo pink. Other characteristic colors include light blue, turquoise, and tropical yellow-green. Lighter and with less of the industrial strength of northern Deco colors, they are nevertheless also derived from sources such as Aztec and Navajo artifacts and exotic tropical birds and flowers.

Color Enhancing Form
Used mostly as accents against the light-reflecting white or cream of stucco and limestone, these colors are only rarely used for the main portion of facades. Most often they appeared as accents to stress the rhythmic repetition of important horizontal or vertical elements and to underscore other geometric devices of Art Deco. Occasionally the local oolithic stone has

The Carlyle, 1250 Ocean Drive, Miami Beach, 1941. Architects Kiehnel & Elliot. The use of strong pastels to highlight vertical and horizontal elements, such as the "eyebrows" over the porch, against white facades is characteristic of the tropical Deco style of hotels and apartment houses of the 1920s through 1940s in Miami Beach. Photo by Susan Russell.

been dyed in matching pink, blue-green, or yellow-cream for use as door trim, balustrades, and applied columns, as has terrazzo flooring of crushed granite mixed with cement.

Integral to the Deco design aesthetic was the burgeoning use of neon, both in the distinctive sans serif sign lettering now used to identify the buildings by name and for interior lighting, usually recessed to provide a reflected glow of soft light. The radiant tones of red or pink, green, and yellow add a final festive touch to the energetic atmosphere of the resort.

Great art is like a tree which grows in a particular place and has a trunk, leaves, blossoms, boughs, fruit, and roots of its own. The more native art is, the more it belongs to the entire world, because taste is rooted in nature. When art is true, it is one with nature.
—Diego Rivera, from *My Art, My Life, An Autobiography*, 1960

49 | Diego Rivera—The Mexican Muralist

Diego Maria Rivera (1886–1957), born in Guanajuato, Mexico, pioneered Mexican murals depicting the social and political history of Mexico in a style of flat, simplified, monumental, decorative forms, which he conjured with bold sweeps of color, a technique which not only contributed to his popularity as

an artist but increased the appeal of the message behind his didactic works.

After traditional training at the official Academia de San Carlos in Mexico City, Rivera received a fellowship to study in Spain from 1907 to 1909, and from 1911 to 1921 he lived

Diego Rivera, *The Agitator*. Mural, Chapingo, Mexico. A cry against the dehumanizing forces of the modern, industrial world, the very Mexican reds and yellows of the protesting peasant (dressed in blue overalls, the universal symbol of the worker) contrasts with the harsh grays of the mine to the right. Sapieha/Art Resource, New York.

and worked in Paris, where he absorbed the avant garde styles such as neo-Impressionism and Cubism. He mastered formal construction by studying Cézanne, but was most influenced by the works of Renaissance muralists such as Piero della Francesca and Michelangelo during a trip he made to Italy in 1920. Invited back to his home country by the Minister of Education following the Mexican Revolution, he returned to Mexico City to participate in a government-sponsored mural program, resulting in his most famous work.

Scourge of the Rockefellers

Rivera was an avowed communist for much of his life, although he executed several murals in the United States; like the revolutionary Constructivists of Russia, he rejected "easel painting" in favor of murals in public buildings, which he felt to be far more accessible to the masses. To appeal directly to the people, he had to dispense with Cubist tricks of distortion and develop a realist, narrative art (which modernists had largely abandoned, but which was related to Soviet Socialist Realism), often depicting events from Mexican history. He borrowed rich colors as well as images from Mexican flora and fauna and pre-Columbian art and was at least partly influenced by Gauguin's dramatic palette.

His first work of 1921 in the Anfiteatro Bolivar of the Escuela Nacional Preparatoria was relatively primitive, a version of the style that would soon come to be known as Art Deco. In fact, throughout the 1920s and 1930s, Rivera's palette revealed Deco elements in his use of bright accent colors, particularly orange, white, and blue against ocher, gray, black, or deep tropical green backgrounds. Less jazzy and elegant than many Deco palettes, Rivera's also included industrial colors, derived from the grimier world of the peasant and factory worker.

Other important works include a series of murals in the Palacio de Cortés, Cuernavaca, for the San Francisco Stock Exchange, and for Rockefeller Center in New York; the latter was destroyed after the artist refused to remove a likeness of Lenin.

Fashion's Theatrics

Often challenging, always dramatic, fashion emerges in the twentieth century as one of the leading media for disseminating new ideas in color. Even as styles and tastes change faster and faster with each passing season, clear directions emerge that link the fashion colors of each decade with prevailing social and economic conditions.

50 | The New Century: Poiret's Exotics

> *I carried with me the colorists when I took each tone at its most vivid, and restored to health all the exhausted nuances.*
>
> —Paul Poiret

Fashion designers have always been receptive to societal and cultural influences, and the French couturier Paul Poiret (1879–1944) was no exception. The bright colors of the Fauve artists of 1905, the extravagant color theatrics of Diaghilev's Russian Ballet of 1909, and the growing freedom of both society and dress after the First World War are all imprinted in his clothing design. The son of a draper, Poiret loved the lively and colorful in art and theater. He inveighed against the Edwardian taste for "swooning mauve," "tender blue," and all that was "washed-out, insipid," and considered "distinguished."

Poiret's silhouettes, like his colors, were radical. His pantaloon skirt, which created a sensation in 1911 and did much to free women from the corset, together with a host of other Poiret designs, are notable for their orientalism, specifically influenced by the costumes seen in Persian and Mughal miniatures, which he collected avidly. Several of his multicolored outfits featured turban hats, often gold in color, and belted, knee-length minaret-inspired tunics, coupled with the narrow silhouette of his harem-like trouser skirts. He further enriched his designs with surface decoration of silver or gold embroidery, as well as beading and fur trim.

Peasant Aesthetics

Under the lasting spell of Leon Bakst's work for the Ballets Russes, Poiret, throughout the 1910s and early 1920s, turned regularly to the dazzling oranges, brilliant blues, and fiery reds—themselves both oriental in influence and drawn from the same Russian peasant costumes that inspired Kandinsky—that had mesmerized Parisian audiences. Yellows and gold tones and blue-greens were typical of Poiret's sensibility, which favored the exotic and bold in color expression, much as the Fauves had.

Poiret's elegant, strongly colored outfits have come down to us primarily

Fall 1917 Forecast, The Textile Color Card Association of the U.S. Dyed silk ribbons. The second seasonal card from an association of American textile manufacturers formed after being cut off from Parisian color direction by World War I. Deep, somber tones reflect the increasing pessimisim about the European war.

through the images of the illustrators such as George Barbier, Erté, A.E. Marty, and Georges LePape, whose work appeared in the new full-color fashion magazines like the *Gazette du Bon Ton*.

Paul Poiret, designs for outerwear and evening dresses, from a limited edition of hand-colored prints by Paul Iribe, 1908. An early example of information on fashion being circulated in full color. Poiret's colors are inspired by oriental sources and predate by a year the famous color theatrics of Diaghilev's Ballets Russes.

The Twenties: Deco Neutrals and Brights

As in the decorative arts, fashion in the 1920s is characterized by a seasonal change in the use of color and the standardization of two colors in particular—black and white—that would remain central to fashion vocabulary for the rest of the twentieth century.

Coming partly in reaction to the explosive fantasies of Poiret and then the Ballets Russes, the first distinct direction was beige, introduced by Coco Chanel in Paris, supposedly to use up army surplus from the First World War. In 1922, she featured slim, tailored skirts woven in pale shades of beige, flesh colored stockings, beige shoes with black toes and heels (to emphasize the length of the leg), and pale colored sweaters, all accessorized with bright costume jewelry, foreshadowing the trend-setting Art Deco palette seen at the Exposition des Arts Décoratifs three years later.

**Art Deco-inspired beachwear designs, 1929.
Courtesy Christine Greiner Designs, New York.**

Multitudes of Whites

Evening gowns appeared in shimmery silks, satins, crepes, and taffetas, all in shades of white—creamy, ivory, or bright white—complemented by a new vogue for pearls and black and white jewelry made from gold, silver, and platinum set with diamonds, crystals, or onyx. The sophisticated neutrals matched the interiors painted with the new titanium whites and including many black (particularly enamel and lacquer) and chrome fixtures. Black, usually combined with white or Deco brights, also began to appear in evening dress at the beginning of the decade, and by the time of the presentations of the 1930 Paris collections, black and white were to predominate.

The House of Worth, one of whose designs is shown here, was the oldest couture house in Paris at the time. It was founded in 1858, by

Lingerie in silk chiffon with lace trim, 1927. Despite the dominance of "machine age" blacks and whites and Art Deco brights, underneath flourished a palette of rich but slightly acid pastels that survived from an earlier generation, the Art Nouveau styles at the turn of the century. Courtesy The Maidenform Museum.

Charles Frederick Worth (1825–1895), the first male couturier to outfit aristocratic women (up until then they had usually been serviced by female dressmakers). He had actually made his mark in the nineteenth century with white, the color required for

Evening gown from the House of Worth, 1921. Typical of the 1920s was the flapper's black dress with colorful accessories, including headband. This was the forerunner of the basic black evening dress still popular today.

formal occasions in France. To make different white gowns for his clients, season after season, he experimented with different fabrications, from silk, tulle, and velvet to brocade, lace, and gauze, showing, as Rei Kawakubo of Commes des Garçons did with black a century later, that there are a multitude of variations within one color. Color accents were provided by trims of gold and silver fringes, or opulent festoons of bold purple violets, vibrant red bows, or clear pink ribbons and detailed appliqués in warm hues. After Worth's death, the business was continued by three successive generations of his family, until 1954, when it became the House of Paquin.

Dress designing . . . is to me not a profession but an art.
—Elsa Schiaparelli

52 | The Thirties: Shocking Schiaparelli Pink

Elsa Schiaparelli (1890–1973) was born into a strict Catholic family in Rome, where her father, a Piedmontese intellectual, headed the Lincei Library. Following a spell in New York after the First World War, she settled in Paris and was aided by Paul Poiret, among others, to develop her skills as a fashion designer. By the 1930s, her vivid colors and unconventional designs had become the rage in Paris and went on to captivate New York after the Second World War. Schiaparelli was strongly influenced by the artists of her time, including the Cubists, the Dadaists, and, most of all, the Surrealists. She used materials freely, even employing cotton for evening gowns and readily accepting the then newly invented synthetic fabrics.

Schiaparelli's collaborative friendship with the surrealist painter Salvador Dali produced some of her most unusual garments, including printed "lobster" and "tear" dresses—the latter, anticipating deconstructivist clothing of the 1980s, accompanied by a torn shawl. Schiaparelli also collaborated with the artist Leonor Fini to bring the world Mae West's hourglass figure in the perfume bottle for "Shocking." Inspired by the Dadaist sculptor and photographer, Man Ray, she created buttons in the shape of lips, which in later evolutions by painter and chemist Jean Clement became mouths, padlocks, butterflies, mermaids, and hands. Another of her artist collaborators was Jean Cocteau, the writer, filmmaker, and visual artist whose whimsical embroidery designs decorated some of the most distinctive Schiaparelli evening dresses and jackets.

Shocking Standard

"Schiap's" color techniques even included airbrushing, a process then generally reserved for the automobile industry. This allowed Clement to produce custom ranges of a color, from which she selected what corresponded to her idea of an

Fall 1933 Forecast, The Textile Color Card Association of the U.S. Dyed wool. Well into the Depression, even the few remaining brights are now modulated, and the card is now dominated by soil-hiding deep tones.

Elsa Schiaparelli, Lobster Dress, c. 1937. White organdy with chiffon cummerbund. Schiaparelli's association with the Surrealists engendered many such flights of fancy and signature brights in her dressmaking, including this lobster-red crustacean on a ground of white, the most important couture color after black. Courtesy The Philadelphia Museum of Art. Given by Mme Elsa Schiaparelli.

"inspired" orange, brown, yellow, green, blue, or red. In 1932, she introduced an ice blue, later a wet moss green, a rose lavender, and a sunlight gold all of which became fashionable after appearing in her designs. Her color hallmark of unexpected shades reached its peak in 1936 with an iridescent cyclamen color, a blend of magenta and pink called Shocking Pink. This became her signature shade and remains one of a handful of fashion colors to become a part of two-hundred textile standards in *The Standard Color Reference of America*, issued by The Color Association of the United States.

LORRAINE WORSTED SHARKSKIN

How glad you'll be to own a suit of
Lorraine sharkskin...pure worsted
sharkskin loomed by top-notch
craftsmen to give you handsome
service for a long, long time. To
be sure of quality fabrics, ask for
fashions of Lorraine worsteds
...at leading stores.

LORRAINE MANUFACTURING COMPANY
INC.
261 FIFTH AVENUE, NEW YORK 16, N. Y.

*Sure-Sized
by Sam Silberstein*

**Worsted Sharkskin Suit, from the Lorraine Co.
Advertisement in *American Fabrics* magazine, 1949.
The tailored look, full skirt, cinched waist, and soft
colors owe a great deal to the lead of Dior's
New Look.**

As a wartime conservation measure and in the interest of National Defense, The Textile Color Card Association has established the policy of reducing the number of colors in all of its collections during the war.
— The Textile Color Card Association, Fall 1942 Forecast

53 | The Forties: Color Rationing

In fashion, the 1940s can be divided into two distinct periods: the war years, with their soil-resistant khakis or olive greens, as well as patriotic reds and blues in boxy military cuts, and the beginning of the post-war boom, coinciding with Christian Dior's "New Look" of 1947, distinguished by the hourglass silhouette, newly voluminous skirts, and soft, feminine colors.

During the war, the American textile industry was closely monitored by the U.S. Government War Production Board, which severely limited access to all fabrics, metal, and leather goods that could be used for military uniforms or equipment. An example of utility wartime attire by ready-to-wear designer Claire McCardell was a basic denim wrap dress that sold in the tens of thousands for a mere $6.95. The industry also voluntarily restricted the number of colors available, effectively suppressing fashion's enormous appetite for new colors, and thus new clothing, every season. (Like the proverbial lump under the carpet, however, color never fully went away, finding an outlet in colorful hats; dancer and singer Carmen Miranda achieved fashion fame for her fruit-piled millinery.)

Shock of the New

In 1947, the "New Look" of Christian Dior (1905–1957) created a sensation, with an exaggerated female silhouette of pronounced bust, figure-hugging waist, and full hips, and mid-calf skirts with hems roughly one foot from the ground. What was particularly shocking, after so many years of shortages, was the amount of material used. A single day dress with an eighteen-inch waist had several yards of fabric in the skirt. Other designs, such as flute-pleated tweeds and evening gowns, were even fuller.

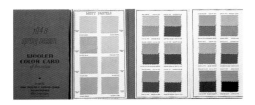

Spring 1948 Forecast, The Textile Color Card Association of the U.S. Dyed wool. Brighter colors are bouncing back from the drabs of the war years; pink is starting to make an entrance, but the palette is still relatively restrained and reflects the returning influence of Paris, particularly Dior's grays and blues.

Not only was the generous use of fine fabrics now a means to express affluence, but so were the light-toned, feminine hues which were far removed from the strong colors of the Deco-inspired pre-war years. Closely associated with Dior are pale grays and blues, colors that recalled the distinguished pales of turn-of-the-century Edwardian styles. More importantly, at a time when not all houses had washing machines, these colors were conspicuously luxurious in that pales, which are easily soiled colors, made for a high maintenance wardrobe.

The Fifties: Pretty in Pastels

The pastels illustrating the 1950s palette were issued in the 1953 Spring Forecast of The Textile Color Card Association of America, a trade organization founded in 1915 to chart American taste in color. The palette is full of "pretty" colors far removed from the drabs of the war years and expressing boundless optimism for American prosperity. The floral names—White Ginger, Blush Camellia, Green Bloom, and Golden Jasmine, among many others—reflected the number one hobby—gardening—of the millions of Americans who were fleeing the cities for the insulated security of the new semi-rural suburban developments.

Signature pastels of the 1950s were pale pink (hot pink, a fully saturated version of it, was also hugely popular), pale blue, maize, amethyst, lilac, seafoam green, and kingfisher blue. The last color, from the German Bayer Company's Alcian dye (introduced in 1951), was the first really clean turquoise dye available to the fashion industry, and, like Perkin's mauve in 1856, became an overnight fashion sensation. Cleaner colors, including pastels, were also appearing in other consumer products from Tupperware bowls to automobile paints (see On-the-Road Pastels, page 124), enabling extensive coordination and cross-fertilization among mediums.

Spring/Summer 1956 Millinery Forecast, The Textile Color Card Association of the U.S. Dyed silk. Hats are still an important fashion item, but their colors are falling into line with the striking pastel palette that is taking off in clothing. The jokey design of this card, based on the shape of a hat box, tells the story of the lively upbeat tone of this decade.

Clean-Cut Colors

In essence, the pastels were soft, clean-cut, innocent, and definitely feminine, only occasionally appearing in menswear and then usually for resort or leisurewear (see Hawaiian Prints, page 123). The palette reproduced particularly well in the fashion magazines (which were using four-color printing technology that was still in its infancy), thus guaranteeing the colors that little extra exposure.

This was a palette of the young or young in spirit, appearing in high school prom dresses, full-circle skirts, and layered sweater sets; but it also found a place in American designer clothing. Bonnie Cashin, who first designed for the Hollywood motion picture industry, introduced her innovative casualwear in the early 1950s, featuring functional layered assemblages in a myriad of colors, largely pastel. The couture designer Charles James (1906–1978), whose ballroom gowns and sculptural capes and coats draped society women, featured pretty pinks, peaches, and cream tones in elegant silk satins, velvets, and chiffons, often contrasting a rose with a pale green or a pale with a bright pink, while the sportswear designer Claire McCardell (1904–1958) created neoclassical nylon evening gowns in peach colors, using a modern fabric in a startling way.

Herbert Sondheim dress, 1952, advertisement in *American Fabrics* magazine, no. 24. Cheery pastels lead off fifties fashion and soon spread to the mass market via the new ready-to-wear industry.

HERBERT SONDHEIM DRESS

*Clouds and clouds of Goldenbro chiffon
made entirely of Enka Rayon yarn . . .
the most enchanting fabric of all.*
*Saks Fifth Avenue; L. S. Ayres, Indianapolis
Neiman-Marcus, Dallas*

AMERICAN ENKA CORPORATION
206 MADISON AVE., NEW YORK 16, N.Y.

KRAMER JEWELRY

55 | The Sixties: Acid Psychedelics

The Italian designer Emilio Pucci (b. 1914) revolutionized what was acceptable in fashionable clothing during the 1950s and 1960s with his flamboyantly vibrant prints and sensuously spare, rule-breaking styles molded to a woman's curves.

Born into an aristocratic Neapolitan family that could trace its roots back to thirteenth-century Florence, Pucci was also a natural athlete, and in 1936 won a skiing scholarship to Reed College in Oregon, where he designed team uniforms consisting of white waterproof cotton knickers, a white parka, a sweater with a big red "R," and a red cap. As a skier, he learned the benefits of clothing that provided freedom of movement, and this became the rationale for his designs for the 1960's jet-setters, bon vivants whose bodies were in perpetual motion. The designs featured elasticized, skin-tight body suits, called "capsulas," of silk and nylon shantung in clashing colors.

Underwater Colors

Pucci's print colors, including "Pucci blue," flame red, magenta, lavender, gold, flamingo pink, acid green, and peach, were inspired by his travels. Many of his 1950's creations were based on hues found in Mediterranean resorts and Tuscan landscapes. He took long sea dives with a camera in hand in order to capture Mediterranean turquoise, coral, and emerald, and he worked closely with chemists and dyers to get the greatest possible vibrancy in his colors. But it was in the way he put the colors together that Pucci broke the conventions for color in dress at the time. To capture some of the explosive energy of a Lichtenstein or Warhol canvas, pinks were swirled alongside ocher yellows, blues were combined with browns, and greens with corals. The whirling and rhythmic patterns, rarely repeated from outfit to outfit, made each garment a unique vision—verging on the hallucinatory—of color movement.

Pucci's images of bright chic and glamor were at odds with the economic and political atmosphere of the 1970s. Yet with the changing tastes of the 1980s and the emphasis on exercise and body revealing clothes, Pucci designs have resurfaced, becoming valuable collectibles treasured for their graphic color appeal.

Emilio Pucci, Dress, c.1960s. Colors inspired by underwater dives in the Mediterranean. Photo by Irving Solero, courtesy The Museum at FIT, New York.

| ## The Seventies: Anti-Fashion Rules

The 1970s seem, in our cultural memory, forever caught between the youth movements of the 1960s and the conspicuous consumption of the 1980s, a drab period between psychedelia and sophisticated reds and blacks. Yet it was a decade with color aplenty, beginning with the ethnic look inspired by the textiles of Russia and Afghanistan, through Laura Ashley's turn-of-the-century pastels in floral prints, and ending with the Day-Glo brights and tartans of the punk rockers.

In interiors, probably the most memorable palette is that of the high-tech look—metal fixtures, plastic furnishings, all colored in industrial-bright primaries in the manner of de Stijl. This palette spilled over into some

areas of clothing, such as the growing market in activewear, in which strong color suggests energy and activity. In general, however, the mood was anti-fashion, even among fashion designers: more natural looks; plenty of peach, yellow, cream, beige, brown, and other earth colors; colors worn layer upon layer; coordinated, but not adhering to any fixed rules.

Among youth, the movement was even more "back-to-basics."

A 1990s interpretation of the 1970s anti-fashion youth look featuring a loose coordination of drab, plaid shirts, and faded blue jeans. Pictured is Maia Halperin.

Replacing the highly tailored or strongly ethnic looks favored by rock musicians of the sixties, a looser youth style appeared. This look featured a layered, thrift-shop look of faded blue jeans, plaid flannel shirts, and soft, "working class" colors of muted primaries together with neutrals. The palette is a northern phenomenon, one of the few in dress that is, almost literally, home grown; the colors evoke the wet and gray

Fall/Winter 1978 Forecast, The Color Association of the U.S. Dyed wool. The forecast card clearly tells the leading color story of the 1970s—rich, strong primary and secondary colors that are appearing in both fashion and product design.

climate of Britain or the northern United States and the soft, misty light conditions that are in strong contrast to Mediterranean-type climates in the south.

Attack Color

Toward the end of the decade, punk became a force and neatly, if surprisingly, synthesized the period's color directions. Caught in tough economic conditions, rebellious and angry, the punks coopted the grungy, working-man's colors and made high style out of tartan trousers and accessories. The bright palette was also recast shockingly out of context, appearing in neon-bright dyed hair and makeup. Mediating between the two color directions and pulling it all together was that emblem of the ultimate rebel without a cause, James Dean, and that dark symbol of sex and tragedy: the black leather jacket.

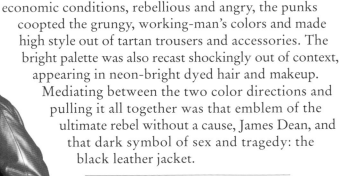

Bonnie Cashin, Red Kid-Leather Coat, c. 1970.
Ultrabright, uncomplicated primaries (in contrast to the 1960s psychedelics) became a major part of the 1970s color story.
Courtesy Bonnie Cashin.

When people ask, "Is that wearable?," it makes me happy because it means it's interesting to them.
—Issey Miyake, quoted in New Fashion Japan, 1984

57 | The Eighties: Japanese Minimalism

Fabric and clothing as concept rather than mere attire startled the American public in the 1980s when pieces by two Japanese designers, Issey Miyake (b. 1938) and Rei Kawakubo (b. 1942), appeared on the fashion scene. Visual themes such as asymmetry, the torn, holey and ragged garment, the encased human torso as a basic silhouette, and, perhaps most importantly, the reintroduction of black and white as key couture colors for the first time since the 1920s, became hallmarks of these two designers. The sculptural qualities of their clothes and their monochromatic palette became the directional fashion statement for the decade.

Miyake took ideas from Japanese work clothes, which had traditionally avoided bright colors, from the kimono, and from other historical costumes and textiles, to create a repertoire of modern forms: oversized, little-cut, rectilinear pieces that loosely wrapped or hung. While on occasion Miyake shot vibrantly bright fuchsias, reds, and acidic greens through his line, Rei Kawakubo and the company she started in 1973, Comme des Garçons, became known for an endless array of blacks. Once, in reply to the question by fashion writer Kennedy Fraser as to why she never used "color" in her collection, her translator replied: "She sees enough color in life."

Ultimately, the story of the 1980s was fabric. Where postwar clothing fabrics through the 1960s were largely cotton, the finer fabrics like silk and linen that were coming back did not seem to require such intense colors. Rei Kawakubo and Issey Miyake were also coming from a long aesthetic tradition that favored earthy, muted (the Japanese called them *shibui*) tones in anything from clothing to ceramics. They showed how simple colors could have infinite variety just as the ancient Greeks had expanded the definition of terra-cotta, how even black or white could be many colors, depending in large part on the fabric. (For instance, blacks in ribbons, chiffon, cotton lace, a wool knit, or silk are perceptually not identical.) By using highly individual weaves and blends in one garment and even employing non-traditional materials such as nickel-plated aluminum or laminated polyurethene/polyester for accessories, they introduced a whole new richness to fashion color and color coordination.

Issey Miyake, Dress, c. 1989. Nature-inspired soft greens and textured browns were also part of the Japanese wave of black and charcoal grays for fashion design. Pictured is Cynthia Nordstrom.

The colors that define the American Century, brilliantly realized in classic consumer products from plastics to tableware, are reproduced in hand-tinted postcards and new four-color printing processes, and finally, coming full circle, canonized by Pop Art in paint.

58 | Hand-Tinted Holiday Postcards

At the turn of century, photographic postcards, which were inexpensive and highly suitable for short messages, became best-selling souvenirs for Americans who were increasingly traveling for their holidays. Enhancing the popularity of postcards during the Edwardian era was the coloring of black-and-white images (full-color photography did not arrive until the 1930s) with photo oil colors and photo painting pencils, which was done both commercially and by enthusiastic holiday-makers.

Color, applied by brush, or through stencils when done commercially, was intended to heighten realism, but the colors used now seem curiously abstract and fantastical, although they were chosen and named to tint specific details in the image: John G. Marshall's manufactured a Tree Green, Sky Blue, Lip Red, Cheek Pencil, and Flesh Pencil; other popular shades included Sandy Beige, Distant Mountain Violet, Sun Yellow, Cloud White, Shadow Gray, and Black. Much of the distinctive charm of the cards comes from these simple colors being put together in strong contrasts that would have pleased Monet—purple and yellow, blue and orange, and so on—with few muddy tones.

All Sweetness and Light

A photo oil is transparent and light in tone so as not to obscure the image. When more opaque shades were desired they could be obtained by adding titanium white; lighter tints were achieved by rubbing down the oil before it dried. The registration tended to blur, since color often bled or stencils overlapped, giving an overall impressionistic softness further enhanced by the rough, matte surfaces of the cards.

The muted hues, so far removed from the brash photographic colors of today's Kodak, Agfa, or Fuji film, are as sweetly artificial as those now used to colorize movies by computer. The sunny palette, grayed only by the underlying black-and-white image, carries on a tradition begun with tinted etchings and lithographs of the second half of the nineteenth century. This process is still used by contemporary photographers seeking offbeat color effects. The palette is essentially a nostalgia piece and, despite its populist origins, advertising has utilized the look of hand-tinted postcards extensively to convey a message of old-fashioned sincerity.

Hand-tinted postcards, c. 1923, depicting New York's Public Library and Brighton Beach. As with hand-colored lithographs of the late nineteenth century, the paints were applied thinly so as not to hide the underlying black image, resulting in characteristically pale tints. Special photo oils thinned with turpentine were applied by brush freehand or, when done commercially, through stencils.

Public Library and Fifth Ave., New York City

Scene at Brighton Beach, N. Y.

| **Bakelite's Consumer Culture**

Bakelite, patented in 1907 and the first successful "true" synthetic plastic, is a revealing example of the transition from one color tradition to another. This palette combines (not without problems) the classic neutrals of the late-Victorian period, browns and creams, with the brights which are the heralds of the modern, consumer age.

Bakelite, like all plastics to follow, never found aesthetic recognition on the merits of its own revolutionary qualities, such as its lightness, strength, and moldability, but instead was stigmatized as an imitation of earlier far more prestigious but costly natural materials such as tortoiseshell, gutta percha (a dark-brown Malaysian resin), and ivory, and was used primarily for throw-away items from brush handles to hatpins. Much effort went into matching natural colorations and effects: swirls of yellow were introduced into the horn- and shell-derived tans, pale-greens, and browns and compressed layers of slightly varying creams reproduced the striations of ivory.

Beginning in 1927, when the Bakelite patent expired, new manufacturers developed brighter yellows, reds, and deep greens that intended no reference to the natural world and did away with swirled effects. These colors are arguably more authentic to plastic, but they are, however, purposefully toned down in deference to prevailing taste. Surprisingly, these softened brights show off bakelite's best aspect—a translucent quality that gives a depth and richness to color that is not easily captured on paper.

The two parts of the palette do not coordinate easily, but they can be used for contrast harmonies in the Art Deco manner, with the brights providing decorative accents; a brash red pattern on a cream ground or green on amber were typical combinations. While the brights had considerable success

Bakelite-handled knives, c. 1920s. From 1927 on, when the original patent expired, Bakelite was forced to augment their line of plastics with strong new colors appealing to Deco taste. Yellows, reds, and greens were enormously popular for items from cutlery to radios well into the 1940s.

on their own in early electronic products such as radios and toys, the most popular colors remained

Bakelite, faux ivory toiletry set, c. 1910s. Early Bakelite carefully imitated the colors and striations of natural tortoiseshell and ivory.

tortoiseshell—which lives on in spectacle frames and fountain pen casings, though now in new plastics—and, above all, black (still a standard for telephones), which effectively hid all impurities in the body of the plastic, although it tended to highlight surface imperfections.

Blue is notable by its absence. This color, which is also rare in natural plastics, except gems, does not flatter the medium and so has been left out of this palette. Its strident tone tends to exaggerate the artificiality of plastic and perhaps for this reason is still often avoided by designers and manufacturers.

The new Harlequin Pottery offers a gift to table gaiety. It brings the magic of bright, exciting color to the tables, dresses the festive board with pleasantness and personality, makes every meal a cheerful and companionable occasion.

—From a Laughlin Co. promotional brochure

60

Harlequin—Dinnerware Brights

The Laughlin China Company, founded in 1871 by Homer and Shakespear Laughlin near East Liverpool, Ohio, and by 1929 operating out of Newell, West Virginia, with continuous tunnel kilns, became America's leading manufacturer of affordable, brightly colored dinnerware in the 1930s, first with Fiesta (1936) and later with Rivera and Harlequin lines (1938). Harlequin was less expensive and thinner than Fiestaware and was sold exclusively by F.W. Woolworth & Co.

The first Harlequin offering featured four colors: lemony yellow (later yellows were of a more primary nature), spruce green, maroon, and periwinkle blue. Designed by Frederick Rhead (1880–1942), an English

Harlequin teapots and miniature figures, c. 1940s. Soft and unusually complex tones, given that they are used for mass-produced tableware. Collection Michael John Wollins.

Stoke-on-Trent potter, the style of Harlequin, like Fiesta, captured the Art Deco spirit of decorative goods in bright colors. Like Fiesta, Harlequin featured bands of rings as ornament. Unlike Fiestaware, though, Harlequin is distinguished by even bands and the absence of a Laughlin company trademark. The 1940s saw the introduction of rose, light green, a red known as "tangerine" (to distinguish it from an identical shade in the Fiesta line called "red"), and turquoise. In the 1950s, dark forest green, gray, chartreuse, and a medium emerald green were introduced. The mid-sixties saw the manufacture of the final pieces in the Harlequin line as initially introduced.

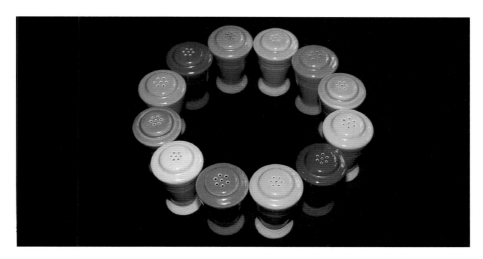

Mix-and-Match Colors

Items in the Harlequin line include teacups and saucers, creamers, sugar bowls, platters, fruit plates, double egg cup, salt and pepper shakers, and drinking tumblers. Harlequin animals were also part of the line during the late 1930s and 1940s, when miniatures were in vogue.

Harlequin salt shakers, c. 1930s –1950s. The complete range of Harlequin colors, which could be mixed and matched by the consumer according to his or her own taste. Collection Michael John Wollins.

One of the great charms of Harlequin was that the consumer could play with color to suit his or her whim. Tables could be graced with a mono-chrome arrangement of only one color, a high contrast of two colors such as maroon and spruce green, or even an assortment of colors that could be randomly mixed, since all the colors harmonized readily with each other.

Assorted Harlequin jugs, c. 1930s–1940s. Rich, slightly off midtones characterize innovative tableware of the Fiesta and Harlequin lines. Collection Michael John Wollins.

61 | Hawaiian Prints—President Truman's Shirt

Hawaiian shirt colors are meant to be highly visible. Known as *aloha* (welcome) shirts, they were primarily a souvenir item for tourists. The colors, like other tropical brights, have to be strong to avoid being visually bleached out by the brilliant sunlight. Rayon, the artificial silk introduced by Du Pont in the 1920s, became the natural choice for fabric because it was cheap and easily took these showy colors.

Appearing before World War II, Hawaiian shirts became a fashion statement on the mainland after the war as a reaction to the years of military tans, olive greens, and navy blues. Glamorized by 1940s and 1950s movie stars like Montgomery Clift and Tony Curtis, they became associated with holidays on new resort islands. They were enshrined as Americana when President Truman, the former haberdasher, was featured in a seagull blue print on the cover of *Life* magazine's December 10, 1951 issue.

The Colors of Paradise

Hawaiian shirt hues are derived from flowers, plants, fruits, and ocean waters. These include anthurium and hibiscus reds, birds-of-paradise oranges, pineapple yellows, surf and ocean blues, evening (reddened) blues, and floral pinks. Shell white was used liberally throughout to set off the colors, having the visual effect of further brightening them. Colors appear singly with white or in intense polychrome groups with clashing hues. Further effects were achieved by reversing print motif and background colors, and a more contemporary image by introducing black for outlines and backgrounds.

The appealing palette of Hawaiian aloha shirts is now more closely associated with children's clothing and food packaging, arenas in which saturated bright colors are perennially popular. In women's and men's apparel, Hawaiian colors and prints enjoy periodic revivals in resort wear. Because the colors, which are more saturated than the Tropical Deco hues of Florida, are dominated by relatively complex, secondary tones such as mint green, turquoise, and purple, the palette has value when a sophisticated bright look is desired.

Hawaiian shirt, c. 1955, with the strident colors inspired by tropical flowers and birds. Casualwear was the only fashion category in which the American male could be persuaded to wear strong colors, and the Hawaiian print became a staple of resorts and barbecue pits alike.

On-the-Road Pastels—Fifties America

Two immediate effects of the end of World War II were the unleashing of a pent-up demand for consumer goods as returning GIs settled into the new suburbs, and the end of America's centuries-long inferiority complex concerning European culture. For the first time a fierce pride in American products swept the nation, and by the early 1950s manufacturers were hard pressed to keep up with demand for "modern" furniture and consumer goods. They were also finding acceptance for new materials such as resin-based plastics and other synthetics which were inexpensive and low-maintenance. Machine-made, often from petroleum products, the new style focused on surface treatments instead of labor-intensive handicrafts such as carving.

As a result, color became increasingly important. Two distinct directions are identifiable. One was the nature-based autumnals (see following section). The other, defiantly "modern," rejected the quasi-naturalistic colors of Bakelite plastics and celebrated instead the candy pinks, mint greens, and turquoises that are forever associated with Formica. The new melamine-based laminate, now easy to color and cheap enough for the mass market (unlike the urea formaldehyde base of prewar plastic laminate), took off in kitchens and diners across America, often in tandem with matching vinyl upholstery. These novel tints embodied the hopes of a world that had put war behind it, or, according to your

1956 Buick two-tone roadster in deep coral and cream. A brief but brilliant flirtation by the automobile industry with more feminine colors. The same colors had been popularized in interiors by Formica with its new laminates.

point of view, symbolized a collective amnesia as America descended into the Cold War.

Roadside diners carried on the same bright pastel colors, beautifully set off by the stainless steel skin and interior fixtures. The Cheyenne Diner, Ninth Avenue and 32nd Street, New York.

The vogue for these colors touched furniture, appliances, automobiles, even office machinery. Instead of generic black, telephones and typewriters started to appear in "feminine" colors such as cream and soft pink, stimulated by the large numbers of women now in the workforce. Textile designers, aided by the new fast vat dyes, explored stronger, larger color masses, often in "shocking" style. For instance, Eszter Haraszty at Knoll introduced the previously taboo combination of orange and pink. Following the lead of Frederick Rhead's prewar Fiesta tableware (1937), furniture designers, such as Charles Eames with his molded plastic chairs, encouraged the consumer to mix-and-match in endless combinations.

In general, however, colors were used singly as a strong design statement. As a result, while they were rich and clear, they lacked subtlety and complexity. Essentially they were tints of the basic hues, red, magenta, green, and blue, lightened so that they all have the same value, or lightness, as a saturated yellow, and thus are easily coordinated. Inevitably, the most successful combinations tend to be of contrasting colors—candy pink with mint green or yellow with blue—often offset by neutral tones of aluminum, stainless steel, or plain black. Suggesting youth and progress, these colors can now seem relentlessly upbeat and playful. However, the palette remains one of the few that clearly demarcate an era, charmingly evocative of a time that used both symbols of atomic energy and biomorphic, amoebal forms as decorative devices.

Of all man-made materials, fabric offers the most and best potential for multitudinous profusion of color.

—Jack Lenor Larsen, Textile Designer

63 | Autumnals in the Fifties

"Bringing the outdoors in" was a popular architectural ploy in the 1950s. Huge plate-glass picture windows blurred the distinction between inside and out, with foliage becoming the backdrop for furnishings. Traditional outdoor materials like flagstone and brick were brought indoors for the warmth and textural interest they could provide, soon followed by landscape colors, particular the autumnals.

These colors, including a vibrant maple red, faded chartreuse green, chestnut orange, and willow yellow, which truly evoke New England fall scenery, are in strange contrast to the atomic motifs of many fabric designs or the spindly legged, "jet-age" furniture of George Nelson and Eero Saarinen. They do, however, complement the wonderfully biomorphic amoebal and boomerang forms of Marco Zanuso's sofas and armchairs and Isamu Noguchi's tables.

Color in Cars

The same indoor/outdoor theme also influenced automobiles, in which for the first time interior and exterior colors were being coordinated. It was here that characteristic two-tone use of autumnal colors appeared, pairing light and dark tones of the same hue—brown and beige, light and dark forest greens, apricot and copper, and so on. Upholstery and trim colors such as yellows, brown-reds, and greens, if not exactly matching, were carefully chosen to complete the woodsy image.

The easy harmonies that these naturalistic colors produce are much more reassuring than the brooding tones of William Morris's nature colors of the previous century. They have experienced a plethora of revivals in clothing and print design. Yet they still have the ability to "lift" an all-white interior and instill a sense of warmth and security in an otherwise bleak environment, just as they did at the height of the Cold War.

Interior for Herman Miller, c. 1950s. The textiles were designed by Alexander Girard and the furniture by George Nelson and Associates. This is a classic example of the other side of the 1950s story—the warmth and homeliness of reds, oranges, and natural woods inspired by the famous fall scenery of the northeastern United States. Courtesy Herman Miller Archives.

Like jazz, comic strips and comic books are quintessentially American. They have had far more influence than usually credited to them: for instance, many of the standard shots used in movies, such as montage, angle shots, panning, and close ups, as well as techniques of compressing time, dialogue, and gesture, originated in comics; and they have anticipated or at least reflected all modern art movements. Pablo Picasso and Lyonel Feininger admitted to being influenced; Joan Miró learned his Escher-like visual logic from Krazy Kat; and in his paintings Roy Lichtenstein reproduced the medium itself.

The dawn of colored comic strips coincided with the development of color printing technology. Richard F. Outcault's "The Yellow Kid" and "Hogan's Alley" both appeared in 1895, in William Randolph Hearst's *New York Journal* and George B. Luks's *The World* respectively, sparking off a circulation war of epic proportions that gave us the term "yellow journalism."

Comic books with extended narratives and simple palettes of muted brights appeared in the midst of the 1930s Depression, quickly replacing the pulp magazines as popular entertainment and showing the way color could be used to create a sequential flow by carrying the same hues and tonal values from frame to frame. The best known artists include Joe Schuster (Superman), Robert Kane (Batman), Tony Abruzzo and Bernard Sachs (Girls Romance), Chester Gould (Dick Tracy), and Russ Heath and Irv Novick, who are known for their war images. Often trashed for unabashed popularism, comics were celebrated by 1960s pop artists Andy Warhol, Jasper Johns, Philip Guston, and Lichtenstein, who with artful simplicity used the same imagery, together with the heightened primary brights and enlarged benday dots.

From Disney Tints to SuperHero Tones
The comic book palette depends on the harsh, largely unmodulated use of basic printers' inks, specifically cyan, magenta, yellow, and black. The colors have gradually moved from simple primaries to more complex shades. They have traditionally been used at strengths of twenty to thirty percent, although comic book artists today are experimenting with ten percent mixes to increase the tonal range made possible by computerized separating and printing technology. Ironically, new techniques and tighter line screens have all but eliminated Lichtenstein's treasured dot patterns.

Spiderman, Comic, 1993. Harsh, updated palette replacing the primary-based Disney pales with secondaries and tertiaries predominating, anchored by the complementary pair of purple and green. In this pop palette of the 1990s, greens have become stronger but are relatively grayed, blues are deeper and richer, and orange is particularly acerbic.

| **Pop Art's Take on Chromotypes**

American corporate culture of the twentieth century has made more use of color symbolism than any group since medieval icon painters. Seeking help in making use of new color reproduction techniques, it has encouraged the emergence of color consulting as a major business, and has responded strongly to modern theories of color psychology (as used in Lüscher and Rorschach tests) and to ideas developed by artists such as Kandinsky and Albers, who argued that color could change the way an object was perceived and might even affect a person's mood.

While identifying logos started to appear in the nineteenth century, color was not an issue until commercial color printing appeared at the start of the twentieth. Kodak yellow, standardized in 1904, was one of the first chromotypes. The company deliberately chose an oranged yellow to represent a sense of light and fun supposedly derived from their cameras and film.

This was soon followed by Coca-Cola red (for energy), American Express green (a symbol of growth and literally the color of American money), and IBM blue (the ultimate color of trust). Very few companies depart from this palette of primary, no-nonsense colors that send a clear message. However, all the colors have been "popped" slightly with a trademark cast. Coke makes use of the ruby red of Gothic stained glass, AmEx green is slightly blue to appeal to conservatives, and IBM used a lightened navy, though this has recently been changed to a near periwinkle to help revamp its image in the 1990s.

Color Subversives

Pop artists of the 1960s onward subverted the whole game of color symbolism. They delighted in mimicking familiar consumer goods, presenting them in a hard-edged, slick style using harsh printing inks applied flat without any of the tonal ambiguities of chiaroscuro. No pop artist was more visible than Andy Warhol, who began as a commercial illustrator before turning to "pop art" and successfully blurring the boundary between art and graphic design. Referring to his studio as The Factory, Warhol argued that the way to success was "to do radical things in a commercial format" and churned out endless multiples of America's icons (soup cans, Coca-Cola bottles, Hollywood stars) as if from a production line, varying only the colorways.

What Warhol was doing with color was not that different from what the Fauves, or, for that matter, the business community, aimed for: all of them sought to elicit a largely emotional response from the viewer. While

Warhol began with product-true colors as in his tomato-soup cans of 1962, he soon flamboyantly digressed into "off" colors—pink, orange, acid yellow, mint green, mauve, and cyan—colors that were consciously non-naturalistic and seemingly influenced by color TV, an innovation introduced in the United States in 1953, and the huge increase in full-color print advertising since the war. Applied quite flat in harsh, ever-changing combinations, they were a rebuke to commerce for appropriating the rich language of color to non-aesthetic ends.

Andy Warhol, *Campbell's Soup,* 1965. Oil silkscreened on canvas. Taking a well-known image from popular culture, Warhol replaces the original red-white-and-black logo with secondary colors, symbolically linking the "can" back to the mass of consumer products—and their characteristic colors—of the fifties, from cars to Formica laminates. Courtesy The Museum of Modern Art, New York, Elizabeth Bliss Parkinson Fund.

Artists' Signatures

Some of the famous palettes of modern artists, who, continuing the work of the Renaissance masters, strove to find inspiration in the incredible new range of paints available to them. From Turner to the Impressionists, from Matisse to the Bauhaus, this was the age of color theory and color experimentation.

66 | Turner's Yellows

J.M.W. Turner (1775–1851), an eccentric figure in the London art world of the early nineteenth century, was frequently the target of ridicule from his contemporaries for his odd social habits and paintings. Nevertheless, he almost singlehandedly revolutionized the use of color in European painting, sowing the seeds of both Impressionism and Expressionism. Particularly in his late pieces, Turner represents the working out in paint of Goethe's theories on color, ideas that he found very compelling.

Himself a competent artist as well as philosopher and poet, Johann Wolfgang von Goethe (1749–1832) decided that Newton's theories of the color spectrum were too clinical and ignored psychological and aesthetic aspects of color. Goethe was more interested in the subjective perception of color. He singled out two colors as being particularly important: blue and yellow, arguing that these represented the two ends of the color spectrum in that they were closely related to black and white (i.e., darkness and light) respectively. Goethe posited that white light turns first yellow when dimmed and then orange (such as when the sun is low on the horizon), red, and finally black; blue comes out black, eventually lightening to white or becoming green when mixed with yellow. Though contrary to most scientific explanations of the light spectrum, Goethe's ideas are a good description of how we actually experience color.

Shock Tactics

Goethe's explanations dovetailed neatly with Turner's own impressionistic observation of the effects of light, although he may not have read Goethe's *Theory of Colors* until after it was translated by his friend Charles Eastlake in 1840. Already by the 1830s, Turner's palette had been narrowed down effectively to yellow, blue, and black, with just touches of red and hints of green. Turner may have been looking for ways to use the brand new, bright and permanent pigments in the blue and yellow range, such as Prussian blue and the chromate, zinc, and cadmium yellows.

While always a great painter of landscapes, toward the end of his life Turner's scenes become less and less recognizable as form dissolved into brilliant and shimmering studies of pure color. His *Fighting Téméraire* shows the basic polarity of yellow and blue in the sun, clouds, smoke, blue sky and sea; Turner's rendition of the old battleship—metaphor for a lost age—being towed in by a steam tug to be broken up, with its fierce and dramatic gestures in color, is like an incarnation of Goethe's words when he urged the reader to "fix a totally yellowish-red surface with one's gaze for the color to seem as if it is actually boring its way into the eye. It produces an unbelievable sense of shock..."

J.M.W. Turner, *The Fighting Téméraire being Tugged to Her Last Berth to Be Broken Up,* 1838. Oil on canvas. The ghostly white ship being pulled by a powerful black tug against the brilliant setting sun represents the end of the age of sail and the arrival of the industrial age . . . and of new, industrial-strength pigments for the artist. Courtesy The National Gallery, London.

67 | **Whistler's Chords**

James Abbott McNeil Whistler (1834–1903), an American by birth, was educated in France and lived as a painter and etcher in London for a significant part of his life. His work presents a wealth of tonal harmonies, and is of particular interest to interior designers because they focus on soft shades rather than specific hues, using whitened and grayed colors in cool and warm tint juxtapositions.

Whistler's style stirred considerable notoriety in his day. In 1877, the art critic John Ruskin denounced *Nocturne in Black and Gold—The Falling Rocke*t, accusing Whistler of "flinging a pot of paint in the public's face." The attack was directed less at his color sense than at his broad, scumbling brushstrokes and evanescent forms merging in and out of the background that foreshadow Monet's *Water Lilies* by nearly a half century. For, whether painting a landscape or portrait, Whistler can be considered by today's standards a subtle colorist, skilled at exploring luminosity and tonal variations; his palette is not at all shocking.

In fact, in an 1885 lecture, Whistler described looking to nature to create his harmonies: "The lessons which Nature presents to the artist alone are of quite a different character. He looks at her flower . . . with the light of one who sees in her choice selection of brilliant tones and delicate tints, suggestions for future harmonies." Harmony and aesthetics, invariably elegant and cosmopolitan, are central to Whistler's portrait of *Valerie, Lady Meux*, which is based around infinite gradations of subtle maroon-browns, pinks, gray-greens, and whites.

Greenery-Yalleries

Whistler was a devotee of Japanese art, and his palette seems greatly influenced by the soft tints of the ukiyo-e prints that had been trickling into western Europe since Commodore Perry dropped anchor in Tokyo Bay in 1853. Above all, Whistler accurately captured the fashionable colors—the delicate tints and off-shades of mauve, green, yellow and white, praised in Gilbert and Sullivan operas as "greenery-yallery" or "cob-webby gray"—that were replacing the brilliant Victorian maroons, purples, and blacks in women's dress toward the end of the nineteenth century.

James Abbott McNeill Whistler, *Valerie, Lady Meux,* 1881. Oil on canvas. Originally called *Harmony in Pink and Gray* (many artists of the late nineteenth and early twentieth centuries, including Kandinsky and Klee, felt that color was subject to laws of harmony analogous to those of music), the painting in fact depends on subtle grayed greens to show off the face and to contrast with the maroon-colored floor. Copyright The Frick Collection, New York.

68 | Monet's Impressions

The Impressionists represents the last gasp of pastoralism in art, which was soon to be changed forever by Cubism. Their landscapes, both rural and urban, were revolutionary at the time, in that they used strong and unusual colors in an attempt to reproduce the effects of light. The Impressionists' choice of color had a lot to do with the range of violent new artists' pigments that were on the market, such as magenta, fuscine (a brilliant purplish red), mauve, cadmium red, cobalt and cerulean blue, and cobalt green. Many

of the Impressionists had also read and internalized the groundbreaking studies by French chemist Michel Eugène Chevreul on the simultaneous contrast of colors, which persuaded them that colors should be applied unmixed, thus unmuddied, on canvases for the greatest visual effect. This led to the signature impressionist style of strokes or dots of pure color to build up an image.

Shown here is the palette of Claude Monet (1840–1926), after whose painting, *Impression, Sunrise* (1872), the movement was named. Monet was supremely

Claude Monet, *Water Lilies*, c. 1920. Oil on canvas. A shimmering miasma of color characteristic of Monet's last years. The artist used colors, principally purples and blue-greens, he used forty years earlier to study the effects of light, and they are here put together to give a sense of water and depth. Courtesy The Museum of Modern Art, New York.

interested in changing light conditions. He is known for several series (such as *Rouen Cathedral* and *Haystacks*) in which he painted the same scene over and over again to explore how colors and light effects change according to the time of day or season of the year.

Dynamic Agitation

In his beloved gardens at Giverny, where he lived after 1885, Monet landscaped a languid, Japanese-inspired garden dominated by a pond that became the subject of his last series, *Water Lilies.* His eyesight failing, he was still able to conjure up a shimmering impression of the scene in his trademark purples and greens. Examining the work up close, one sees the dynamic agitation of his brushstrokes, exemplifying his regret that he could never paint fast enough. "I want to paint the air which surrounds the bridge, the house, the boat: the beauty of the air in which these objects are located, and that is nothing short of impossible." Yet, seen from normal viewing distance, *Water Lilies* is charmingly tranquil, a wall of harmonious color.

Other notable Impressionists include Pierre-Auguste Renoir (1841–1919), Alfred Sisley (1839–99), and Camille Pissaro (1830–1903). Typically, the impressionist palette excluded black and white, using only the brightest oil pigments of yellow, orange, vermilion, red, violet, blue, and intense green, such as Veronese and emerald, mostly used in the coolish harmonies they found in the northern French landscape.

69 | Seurat's Points

French neo-Impressionist painter Georges Seurat (1859–1891) is credited, along with Paul Signac, with developing pointillism, a technique of applying paint in tiny dots in an attempt to be more scientific in the process than the earlier Impressionists. Seurat was also preoccupied with the effects of light, but, unlike his predecessors, he avoided painting *en plein* air, and his paintings have the studied look of months of careful dabbing indoors in his atelier.

Seurat carefully juxtaposed pure colors so that the eye of the viewer would visually mix the colors. In this way he hoped to achieve the brightest possible color in his paintings. Unfortunately for him, although his small points of color do blend optically at normal viewing distances, the complementaries he used, rather than enhancing each other, tended to cancel themselves out to produce grayish shades, just as benday dots in the printer's three primaries mix to produce gray. The Fauvists, using broad swathes of color, had far greater success at creating a sense of vivid hues.

Gray Moods

This graying is now seen as part of the charm of pointillism and can heighten the mood effects that Seurat sought to create in paintings such as *Invitation to the Sideshow*. This is a startling rendition of the chilling effects of artificial light. The atmosphere created by the dulled green and purple is one of melancholy, which the shimmering appearance of the gaslight only heightens. In contrast, the softening of the greens and yellows in the familiar *A Sunday Afternoon at the Grand Jatte* helps to create a mood of still well-being.

The grainy effects and the softly graded tonal ranges that Seurat achieved resemble those of the earliest color photographs (such as the turn-of-the-century autochromes developed by the Lumière brothers), a quality that some photographers seek to reproduce today. Textiles, too, which routinely use color in small-scale patterns to create heathered or textured looks, can achieve the same sober tones with mixtures of brighter colors.

Note that the palette shown here aims to capture the overall effect of Seurat's palette only, not the individual colors, which are closer to being fully saturated.

Georges Seurat, *Invitation to the Sideshow* (La Parade de Cirque), 1887–89. A melancholy, gaslit gloom descends on a Parisian evening, captured with Seurat's distinctive pointillist method, showing how even the purest colors can be dulled by the influence of their neighbors. The Metropolitan Museum of Art, Bequest of Stephen C. Clark, 1960. (61.101.17) © 1989 by the Metropolitan Museum of Art

How do you see this tree? Is it really green? Use green, then, the most beautiful green on your palette. And that shadow, rather blue? Don't be afraid to paint it as blue as possible.
—Paul Gauguin, to Paul Sérusier, a young disciple

70 | Gauguin's Primitives

The French-born painter and sculptor Paul Gauguin (1848–1903) had a profound impact upon the development of post-impressionist art and subsequent color design. He liberated color from its descriptive function to create symbolic abstracts of geography and culture. In *Vision After the Sermon* (1888), painted in Brittany, he depicts praying Breton women in rustic yellowed whites, intense blacks, ultramarine blues, and striking vermilion ground; during his Tahitian period the warm exotics common to native art and dress of that tropical island were central.

Several factors influenced Gauguin's remarkable colorations. One was an interest in Japanese art and its stylized use of color. Another was his ceramic work with Ernest Chapelet (1835–1909), which taught him to simplify and order shapes and color in order to "synthesize" for meaning or to invoke an image. Perhaps the most influential factor came from the artist's own quest for exotic or, in his own words, "savage and primitive" splendor; this led him from Paris to Brittany in 1886, then to Martinique in 1887, and finally to Tahiti in 1891.

Barbaric Luxury

To capture the opulence of Tahiti, Gauguin used pure bright pigments— vermilion, chrome yellow, cobalt blue, and emerald green—against rich, reddened tropical earths, greenish brown skin tones, and blued shadows. His brilliant but moody palette was hugely influential on later art, from the dense, purplish browns of Picasso's early works to the harsh dissonances of red, yellow, and green of Matisse. In deference to primitive art, Gauguin also boldly outlined the figures in his paintings, often in Prussian blue rather than black—to pop them from the background. This isolating and thus brightening of colors was also an old European technique (*cloisonnism,* as the French called it, from their word for division) that began with medieval enamel work and stained glass, and was also a feature of Japanese prints, with their hard outlines filled in with relatively flat colors.

During the last years of his life in Tahiti, a period of enormous productivity, Gauguin found the freedom for

Paul Gauguin, *The Moon and the Earth* (Hina Te Fatou), 1893. Oil on canvas. Not only the imagery but also the deep, brooding colors, punctuated with harsh greens and reds, are drawn from Gauguin's experiences living on the tropical French colony of Tahiti. Courtesy The Museum of Modern Art, New York, Lillie P. Bliss Collection.

dramatic variation and experimentation with colors, although always in terms of the culture within which he was living and working (and, incidentally, which he felt was being destroyed by Western culture). As he put it in a letter discussing one of his paintings, *Nevermore*, "I wished to suggest by means of a simple nude, a certain long-lost barbaric luxury. It is completely drowned in colors which are deliberately somber and sad; it is neither silk, nor velvet, nor muslin, nor gold that creates this luxury, but simply the material made rich by the artist."

71 | Kandinsky's Spirituals

The Russian painter Wassily Kandinsky (1866–1944), was the intellectual godfather of abstract art. Author of *Concerning the Spiritual in Art* (1912), he was, for most of his life, an ardent follower of the spiritualist Madame Blavatsky. An early cult leader, Blavatsky prophesied that the material world would soon come to an end and be replaced by a world of the spirit in which people would communicate in "thought forms." Kandinsky believed that color was such a form. As a result, he felt that colors should be used in art purely for their emotional and symbolic content (just as they were in Russian icons) and not for their representational accuracy. This became a key idea in the development of abstract art.

Early on, Kandinsky indicated his commitment to color and to its expressionistic potential. In 1889, on a trip to the Russian provinces, he had been struck by the intensity of the peasants' untutored color sense. In 1895, when he was twenty-nine and had not yet given up his law career, he saw Monet's impressionistic *Haystacks*, and wrote of "the unsuspected power, previously hidden from me, of the palette," claiming that "the object was discredited as an indispensable element of the picture." For Kandinsky, and for later Expressionists, what was portrayed was of less import than the viewer's emotional and spiritual reaction to the painting.

The Color of Music

Looking for something like a unified theory of art, Kandinsky equated colors with basic (abstract) forms—red with a square, blue with a circle, yellow with a triangle—and with musical tones, developing an idea that had been around since Newton identified the seven colors of the spectrum with a diatonic scale. According to Kandinsky, red rang like a trumpet or thundered like a drum; yellow sounded like a shrill bugle note; blue was an inward color, having a cello-like sound, or, at its darkest that of an organ; green was a restful color like the middle notes of a violin.

Of all the colors, according to Kandinsky, blue (that favorite of stained glass makers and icon painters) was the most spiritual, and thus the most significant, as in the *Blue Mountain* from which this palette is extracted. Not yet fully abstract, this piece incorporates images of horses and riders, but these figurative elements have less of an impact than the brooding, primary blue, red and yellow masses that dominate the canvas. The effect is like a chord of color harmony, with the three primaries in perfect balance and subtly enriched by the minor key of orange, purple, and green.

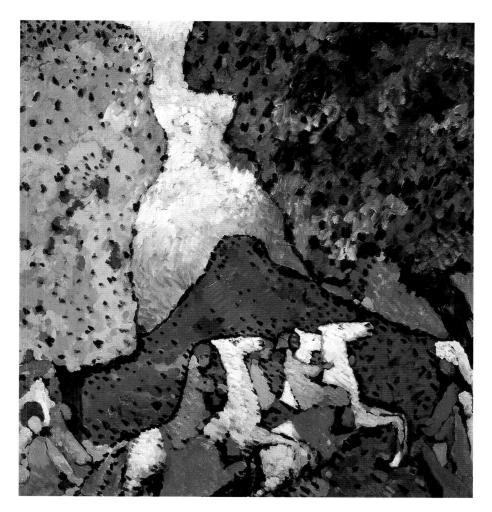

Kandinsky's palette is in stark contrast to the monochromes of the Cubists, who were becoming celebrities at the time, but who, moving in a different direction, believed color subverted their purposes. However, his palette is very much of its time, a period that encompassed the exotic colors of Gauguin, the brash color statements of the Fauves, and the theatrics of Paul Poiret and Leon Bakst (for the Ballet Russes), soon to evolve into the glitzy glamour of Art Deco.

Wassily Kandinsky, *Blue Mountain*, 1908–09. Oil on canvas. A study of the expressive effect of the three pigment primaries, red, yellow, and blue, the last being the most "spiritual." The palette is remarkably similar to that used in another field by couturier Paul Poiret in 1908. Courtesy Solomon R. Guggenheim Museum, New York. Gift Solomon R. Guggenheim, 1942. Photo by David Heald, © The Solomon R. Guggenheim Foundation, New York.

| **Klee's Grids**

Paul Klee (1879–1940) was an unusually prolific artist who turned out more than four-thousand pictures in a variety of media from watercolor to oil. Of these, however, more than half are plain pen-and-ink drawings, underscoring the fact that he was first an accomplished cartoonist before he became a great colorist, which makes his work particularly instructive to the graphic designer. Well into his early career he struggled to reconcile his line with color, confiding to his diary in fits of depression his fear that he would never learn to control and use color, and thus would never be a painter.

Determined to overcome this perceived weakness, he studied the work of Delaunay, translating his *On Light* into German, and worked with Kandinsky, August Macke, and Franz Marc. On a trip to Tunisia in 1914, he experienced a breakthrough that allowed him to say, "Color and I are one, I am a painter." His trick was to develop a grid (a technique also used by the Cubist and de Stijl artists) to break down natural forms into their component shades and colors. He started applying colors in rough rectangular shapes that only loosely corresponded to the framework of the painting and which became the heart of his work.

Klee's Key

These boxes of color, enlarged versions of pointillist dots, provided a structure to study sequences, as well as the overall effect of color independent of any strict representation. Increasingly, influenced by Kandinsky's theories of color and music, Klee identified the boxes with musical notes, and saw himself as a composer who used color. In fact, his hobby was playing in a string quartet. Throughout much of his career, Klee's palette works like a musical scale: while he has a huge range, certain colors keep coming back as if a favorite key. These include most notably a mint green, a coral, an ocherish yellow, a siena red/pink, and some very distinctive blues ranging from reddish to greenish, brights that, as with Matisse, may have been influenced by his time in North Africa.

Accompanying—or rather lingering behind—this palette is a range of somber neutrals which suggest Klee's dark and melancholy side, especially after the deaths of his friends Macke and Marc in the Great War. Klee's 1918 painting *Out of the Gray of Night There Once Emerged . . .* , built around the letters of his own poem, summarizes the way he used color, building up out of these dark tones and never wholly leaving them behind. Often bright and puckish (as one might expect of his cartoonist side), his colors are always being tamed by the somber deeps.

The palette, with its controlled and simple color scales, is very applicable to graphics and to computer art and design:

Paul Klee, *They're Biting*, c. 1920. Oil on canvas. Klee's characteristically earthy and slightly acidic colors. Difficult to pin down, they merge in and out of each other and out of black. Tate Gallery, London/Art Resource, New York.

both the sweet and the dark colors are surprisingly good looking on a computer monitor and easy to reproduce by four-color printing. Similarly, Klee's technique for breaking down a design into discrete color boxes suggests possibilities for eliminating the punishing monotony of computer-generated color.

73 | **Modigliani's Mistress**

Italian artist Amedeo Modigliani (1884–1920) is noted for his idiosyncratic, rather mournful portraits, particularly of Jeanne Hébuterne, his companion for the last three years of his short life. Working in Paris starting in 1906, he was strongly influenced by the African sculpture then being collected; elongated necks and bodies (which also refer discretely to mannerism) together with empty eye sockets, became his signature motifs.

His harmonies, however, suggest the influence of Sienese art and the fresco tones of Piero della Francesca. In fact, he often consciously ignored the glazing possibilities of oil, applying the paint with dabbing strokes that would more normally be used with fast-drying tempera paints. As a result, the simple, flat color zones that have an abstract force of their own also have an appealing texture that contrasts with and thus highlights the finely rendered faces and hands.

Sky-Blue Eyes
The colors themselves are muted and unaggressive. His *Jeanne Hébuterne with Yellow Sweater* (1918–19), painted shortly before his (and her) death, is based around an earth palette of siennas, umbers, and a malachite green that would not be inappropriate to a fifteenth century Italian church. (Modigliani often also used the smallest possible touch of a Piero-like sky blue as an accent in the eyes.) Modigliani shows again how beautiful the earth palette can be in a modern setting, particularly if applied with plenty of texture and how color can be used expressively, without having to resort to the theatricality of brights.

Amedeo Modigliani, *Reclining Nude,* c. 1919. Oil on canvas. Displayed is Modigliani's idiosyncratic palette of maroon, ocher yellow, and orangy flesh tones, colors associated with the African art from which he drew inspiration for his portraits. Courtesy The Museum of Modern Art, New York, Mrs. Simon Guggenheim Fund.

The triumphant colorist has only to appear. We have prepared his palette for him.
—Paul Signac

74 | Matisse's Beasts

Few painters, past or contemporary, are as well known simply for their color as the French artist Henri Matisse (1869–1954). Since the blockbuster exhibition, *Henri Matisse: A Retrospective,* at The Museum of Modern Art in New York in 1993, he, along with Van Gogh and Picasso, has become one of the world's most popular and visible painters.

A leading figure among the Fauves and later the synthetic Cubists, Matisse is perhaps most associated in the public's mind with vibrantly colored cutouts, the free-flowing paper works of his final years. Yet his work of the 1900s clearly prefigures that of the 1950s. Pictures are reduced to their basic elements—blocks of color, hard lines, shapes reduced to their simplest components, images that flit between being clearly representational and looking more like an allover pattern on a bright wallpaper. Color is the common denominator—bright, lava-like, lurid, uncluttered, an inspiration for the American Abstract Expressionists.

Whether painting in the harsh light of the south of France, which he did increasingly after 1905, or in his shed at Issy-les-Moulineaux just outside Paris, Matisse was unwavering in his Fauvist commitment to strong color. Rather than use it naturalistically, he preferred to develop seemingly arbitrary sequences and combinations—blue-green, maroon, bright blue, yellow-green, scarlet, orange, and ocher—which infuriated critics in Paris and New York who cried "wild beast" (in French, *fauve*), but which expressed his own personal vision of harmony.

Carving Color

Matisse's strongly graphic, even decorative, arrangement of color was to last his lifetime. It found a compelling outlet when, confined to bed after a serious operation in 1941 and unable to use an easel, Matisse turned to making paper cutouts. Paralleling Albers's experience with paper at the Bauhaus (see page 90), he was fascinated with the ultimate flatness of the medium whose essence was color, not three-dimensional modeling. "To cut right into color makes me think of a sculptor's carving into stone," he wrote of his new art, which was to influence a generation of graphic designers.

Matisse's palette includes a signature blue, accent oranged red, and flesh beige tones (these hues appear equally extensively in Coptic textiles, which he admired). While color so often goes from edge to edge, Matisse often left areas of the canvas unpainted so that the white would provide a glistening contrast to the saturated hues. For graphic and textile designers, his work has not dated at all and still presents full-blown, charged colors in perfect balance—upbeat combinations that still surprise but no longer shock.

Henri Matisse, *Goldfish and Sculpture*, 1912. Colors reflect
Matisse's exposure to Moorish tiles during his visit to
Morocco, as well as his interest in Expressionist ideas. The
palette is one to which he would keep returning all his life.
Note how the colors are balanced according to their visual
weight, from large areas of passive blue to touches of strong
red. Courtesy The Museum of Modern Art, New York, Gift
of Mr. and Mrs. John Hay Whitney.

Ethnic Sources

Ending where we began, some of the oldest palettes in the world can provide combinations as subtle and sophisticated as any developed in this century. These are the color schemes, whether earthy in tone or tropical bright, that have withstood the test of time by being perfectly adapted to their environment.

75 | India's Subtropical Brights

Pink is India's navy blue.
—Diana Vreeland

Tropical and subtropical regions have often featured exotic brights in clothing and architecture, and have welcomed the new synthetic dyes and pigments of the twentieth century. These are the colors, used at full saturation, that best stand up to glaring sun and deep shadows. Because they are all of roughly the same intensity, colors in otherwise unusual combinations such as turquoise and ultramarine, red and fuchsia pink, can in fact harmonize readily. Few Indian colors are as simple as the stark primaries used in the West; each tends to have a distinct color cast—a bluish tinge in greens, a reddish tone in blues, distinctly orangy reds and strident purplish pinks.

Indian skill with manipulating bright color dates back to pre-history and the discovery of mordants, the metallic salts that help dyes penetrate the textile fiber. By using different mordants, a range of colors can be obtained from a single dye. Kermes, obtained from a tree-dwelling scale insect and known for its reds (numbering several dozen distinct shades), can also produce cool pink, peach, brown, purple, black, and even green tones. Other principle dye sources include lac and madder (reds), turmeric and saffron (yellows and oranges), safflower (yellows and pinks), gambier and catechu (yellows and browns), and indigo (blues).

Because of India's success in dyeing, bright color has permeated the culture and religion well before the arrival of western synthetic dyes and has long been charged with poetry, symbolism, and romance. Gods are portrayed in primary colors: blue for Krishna, yellow for Vishnu, red for Lakshmi, and so on; celebrants at the festival of Holi sprinkle each other with intensely colored powders; brides are sprinkled with turmeric; centuries ago, even Buddhist monks took to wearing saffron robes—an act of humility akin to European monks wearing drab browns and blacks, since yellow is the color of the earth and was worn by prisoners. Brilliant color, as far removed from the earth tones as possible, becomes a sign of a civilized, not a primitive, culture.

Contemporary blouse, c. 1970, worn by young Rabari women for festivals, Gujurat, India. The blouse is characteristic of the bright colors (now derived from synthetic dyes) typical of India, where they stand up well to the strong and relatively unchanging, subtropical sun. Courtesy Barbara Arlen Associates, New York.

| **Asian Tie-Dyes**

Tie-dyeing is a classic way of applying color and pattern to cloth, easier than weaving and thousands of years older than printing. The simplicity of the process has allowed the practice, which may have begun in Asia, to spread throughout India, Malaya, Indonesia, and Africa. It was even used independently in the Americas, such as among the Pueblo Indians of the southwestern United States.

Characterized by a cracked and marbled appearance, tie-dyes tend not to be too bright or saturated in appearance. The surface effects are based on resist techniques where dye is prevented from entering parts of the fabric. A relatively advanced resist method is that of batik, where hot wax is used to "paint" on a pattern; in the dye bath, the wax literally "resists" the dye. In tie-dyeing, the cloth is tightly knotted, or folded and tied with waxed string, before it is dipped in the dye bath. The pressure of the knots or the string keeps the dye off, and when dried, the cloth has a unique pattern of rings and lines. The patterns can be altered infinitely by the number of ties (up to thirty per inch) or by tying pebbles, wood, or seeds into the cloth.

Multicolored effects can be achieved by submersing portions of the cloth into a different dyebaths, or, occasionally, by second immersions. Generally, however, tie-dyes are monochromatic, with the undyed, or white parts providing the pattern. Traditional sources of color are natural plant dyes, available locally, and patterns varied from region to region. Largely defunct with the arrival of modern printing techniques, tie-dyeing did have a brief revival in America in the sixties, when it was prized by a generation of hippies for its irregular, hand-crafted look.

Tie-dyed silk chiffon scarf by Aminaben, Gujurat, India. Courtesy Barbara Arlen Associates, New York.

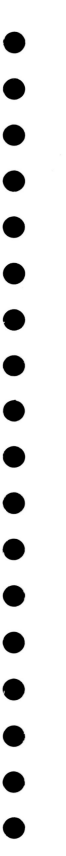
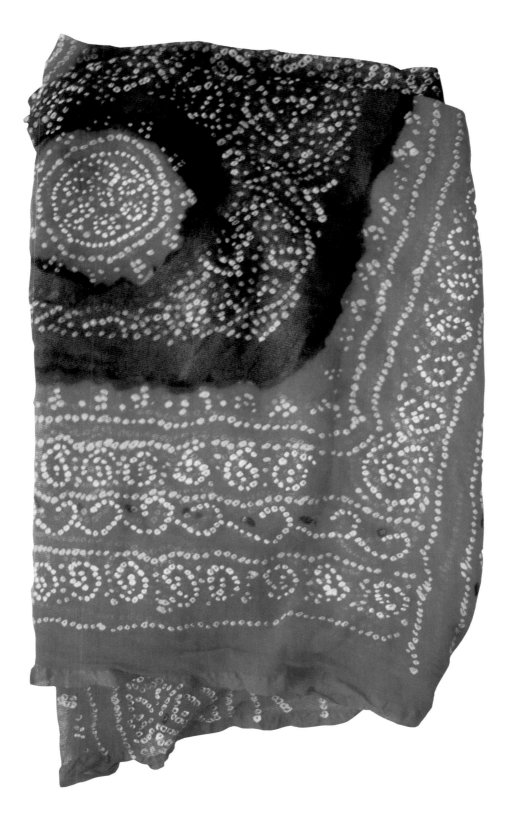

| **Peru's Warm Harmonies**

Deeper in tone than the Guatamalan palette, the Peruvian palette is characteristic of the Andean region of South America. Earliest dates place the development of woven cotton textile production to 2500 BC, with woolen fabrics, from the domesticated llama and alpaca as well as the wild vicuna, developing later.

The Andean weavers of Peru tended to contrast vivid colors, particularly red, blue, yellow, brown, and cream. Different shades of the same hue, such as a red and a pink or a light and dark blue, enriched simple geometric motifs. Figurative motifs commonly included pumas, fish, birds, flowers, and plants, all represented in a manner almost as stylized as in kilim designs. The figures were often produced, or outlined, in concentric lines of different colors, creating a sense of movement within the otherwise static and stylized forms.

Peruvian designs incorporated wool's natural whites, grays, browns, tawny oranges, and black. Dyes derived from plant and vegetable matter of the region included yellows, dark browns, blues, purples, greens, white, and black. The multilayered color style and repeating images allowed for the development of intricate patterns and the display of many shades (up to 190 in a single fabric have been distinguished) in pre-Columbian textiles of the two great Pan-Peruvian cultures, Tiahuanaco (AD 600–900) and Inca (AD 1100–1530).

Peruvian Huari-style tunic detail. Courtesy The Textile Museum, Washington, D.C., 1961.3.17.

Peruvian Huari textile, Tunic fragment.
Pre-Columbian. Courtesy The Textile
Museum, Washington, D.C., acquired by
George Hewitt Myers.

The vibrant reds, pinks, and oranges, interwoven with the vivid blues, purples, and hints of acidic greens and yellows of Guatamala are the most visible survivors of a Mayan culture that has barely clung to existence since the arrival of the Spanish Conquistadors and the spread of Christianity. These are the iridescent colors of the central American tropical jungles, of arrow-poison frogs, parrots, and sacred quetzal birds, and thus, by extension, of the gods of early animistic religions, many of whose rituals and symbols still survive today.

Coloring agents used in pre-Columbian Guatemala, and relatively common up until the 1970s, were derived from mineral and vegetable substances and used traditionally to dye cotton, although wool and imported synthetic fibers are now also used. Colorants include charcoal (black), iron hydroxide (yellow), cochineal, Brazil nuts, and achiote spice (reds), the sacatinta plant and clay (blues), nance (a cherry-like fruit) and the aliso tree (dark browns), and sometimes the mollusc purpura patula (purple, a highly prized color). Synthetic dyes have now added characteristic acidic greens and yellows.

Generally colors are combined into multicolored patterns in the weaving process, which is still done in some remote areas on the original backstrap loom. Distinct patterns identify the weaver or wearer as belonging to a specific cultural group, and are also artistic interpretations of the natural world. Guatamalan colors evoke images of the weavers' life-supporting surroundings: a vibrant green might suggest an unripe banana; a yellow set against a red background conjures the energy of the sun. Colored fibers are woven to create stripes, geometric patterns, and symbols such as the sun and moon, stylized animals, double-headed eagles, and the plumed serpent god—Quetzalcoatl in Aztec and Toltec cultures—that preserve the Mayan legacy.

Embroidered handwoven cotton scarf from Quezaltenango, Guatemala, c. 1920. A late example of a fabric using natural dyes; by the 1970s most Guatamalan products had switched to modern synthetic dyes. Courtesy Barbara Arlen Associates, New York.

| **Mineral Tones of the Southwest**

The landscape and architecture of the American Southwest, particularly New Mexico, is dominated by the soft, cool, and variegated browns of traditional adobe, the sun-baked bricks used to build the pueblo communities from Acoma to Taos. Adobe architecture's sculptural forms still define the look of New Mexico, and adobe is used extensively for residential housing throughout the state's capital, Santa Fe, and at the University of New Mexico at Albuquerque, the state's largest campus.

Since the earthtones blend so naturally into the scrubby desert landscape, parts of the buildings, such as entrances and windows, are often highlighted with an accent color, particularly white and blue or blue-green. This color of turquoise beads is one of the most significant colors to the Navajo and Pueblo Indians of the region, who, long before the arrival of the Spanish, considered it to be a sacred color that could guard them against mishaps, just as a cobalt blue did in the Middle East. The Christian tradition in religious art of associating blue with the Virgin Mary was fortuitous, as it encouraged the Pueblo use of blue to survive into modern times.

Adobe church, New Mexico. Colored in soft earthtones with accents of white that prevent it from completely vanishing into the landscape.

Pueblo, Zuni, Hopi and Navajo textiles are the source of the other part of the southwestern palette—white, gray, red and black—originally used on cotton and then on wool

Covered walkway, Santa Fe, New Mexico. A traditional turquoise drawn from the semi-precious stones used in local Navajo jewelry.

with the introduction of sheep by the Spanish. Traditional (i.e., pre-Columbian) textile colors were largely confined to brown, white, and a grayish indigo blue; red was only added during the late eighteenth century (when it gradually replaced blue). With no locally available dye for this color, red threads were obtained by unraveling and respinning pieces of bayeta, an English flannel cloth imported by the Spanish.

80

The Universal Mudtones

Ultimately, all color comes from the earth, and mudtones, the oldest colors used by man to paint art and decorate his environment, still maintain their primeval power. They include red from iron-rich earth, yellow from ocher, black from soot and charcoal, white from lime and chalk, and a host of intermediate grays and browns. The same palette continually reappears in all parts of the world, in all climates, and in many stages of civilization, from tribal Africa to ancient Greece, from Pueblo Indian America to Edwardian England. And for good reason.

In a classic linguistic study by two American anthropologists, Brent Berlin and Paul Kay, it was discovered that black, white and red are always the first colors to be named in any primitive language, with yellow coming in fourth. Not only are these the easiest colors to reproduce, but they also carry the greatest symbolic weight. Black and white represent the basic perceptual division between darkness and light, night and day; red is forever associated with the life force, with blood itself. And so it goes on. In many cultures, especially in Africa, black is identified with earth, masculine qualities, and material matters; white is heavenly, spiritual, and feminine; and red represents sexuality.

Using these colors, the early painter, portraying the hunt on cave walls, could make magic, hoping to control the mysterious forces that defined his existence. The face painter preparing for religious rituals would use the same colors to express qualities in himself

Mudtones: Hopi earthenware bowls.

Petroglyph from West Mesa, Albuquerque, New Mexico.

and thus define his position in society, just as we define ourselves even today with dark blue or gray business suits or plumage-bright athletic wear. "Face painting," said Claude Lévi-Strauss, the French anthropologist, "indicates the passage from nature to culture; the painted face is a sign of the civilized man."

Ultimately, these are the colors—light, dark, and ruddy—that provide the strongest effect, not just for the mud-printer or pictograph painter, but also for those of us peopling a high-tech world that is being swamped, thanks to advances in color reproduction, with all the colors of the spectrum.

Color Palettes